Reading Shakespeare Today

HAMLET

Caitlyn Christensen

Cavendish Square
New York

Published in 2016 by Cavendish Square Publishing, LLC
243 5th Avenue, Suite 136, New York, NY 10016

First Edition

CPSIA Compliance Information: Batch #CW16CSQ

Cataloging-in-Publication Data

Christensen, Caitlyn.
Hamlet / by Caitlyn Christensen.
p. cm. — (Reading Shakespeare today)
Includes index.
ISBN 978-1-5026-1034-8 (hardcover) ISBN 978-1-5026-1035-5 (ebook)
1. Shakespeare, William, — 1564-1616. — Hamlet — Juvenile literature. I. Title.
PR2807.C475 2016
822.3'3—d23

Editorial Director: David McNamara
Editor: Andrew Coddington
Copy Editor: Rebecca Rohan
Art Director: Jeffrey Talbot
Designer: Stephanie Flecha
Senior Production Manager: Jennifer Ryder-Talbot
Production Editor: Renni Johnson
Photo Research: J8 Media

The photographs in this book are used by permission and through the courtesy of: Jupiter/Photolibrary/Getty Images, cover; Shutterstock.com, front, back cover and background throughout the book; Oli Scarff/Getty Images, 5; Peter Phipp/Britain On View/Getty Images, 6; Art Media/Print Collector/Getty Images, 9; Universal History Archive/UIG via Getty Images, 12; Superstock, 14; Nat Farbman/The LIFE Picture Collection/Getty Images, 18; File: File-Hamlet, Prince of Demark Act I Scene IV. by Henry Fuseli/ Digital ID, cph.3c15274/Library of Congress/Prints and Photographs/Wikimedia Commons, 20; Hulton Archive/Getty Images, 25; TWO CITIES/RANK/Album/Newscom, 26; Hamlet attempts to make Guildenstern play a pipe, from 'Hamlet' by William Shakespeare, edition published by Hodder & Stoughton in 1915 (colour litho), Simmonds, W. G. (20th Century)/Private Collection/Bridgeman Images, 30; Le Roi Lion (The Lion KIng) de RogerAllers et rob Minkoff avec les personnages de Simba et Scar, 1994./Photo © RDA / Bridgeman Images, 33; AF Archive/Alamy, 34; File: Edwin Austin Abbey, The Play Scene in Hamlet, 1897/Wikimedia Commons, 37; File: Richard Dadd - Hamlet and his Mother; The Closet Scene - Google Art Project/ Wikimedia Commons, 43; File:John Everett Millais - Ophelia - Google Art Project.jpg - Wikimedia Commons, 47; Hulton Archive/Getty Images, 49; Mondadori/Newscom, 52; Ronald Grant Archive/Mary Evans Picture Library Ltd/Age fototock, 55; Denis Charlet/AFP/Getty Images, 59; File: Wladyslaw Czachórski Actors before Hamlet, 1875/Wikimedia Commons, 60; Ullstein Bild/Getty Images, 62; Donald Cooper/REX/Newscom, 67; Hulton Archive/Getty Images, 71; Donald Cooper/REX/Newscom, 73; Moviestore Collection Ltd /Alamy, 76; File: Mignon Nevada as Ophelia/Bain News Service/Library of Congress/Wikimedia Commons, 78; CASTLE ROCK ENTERTAINMENT/Album/Newscom, 81; File:Claudius at Prayer Hamlet 3-3 Delacroix 1844.JPG - Wikimedia Commons, 83; Courtesy Islinglass Theater, Portland, Oregon, 91

Printed in the United States of America

CONTENTS

Introduction

SHAKESPEARE AND HIS WORLD

William Shakespeare is a towering figure in English literature. Centuries after his lifetime, it is difficult to go long without encountering "The Bard" in some way, shape, or form. A prolific playwright, he is credited with writing 38 plays and 154 sonnets. His plays, such as *Romeo and Juliet*, *A Midsummer Night's Dream*, and *Macbeth*, continue to be performed on stage, depicted in films, and referenced in popular culture. *Hamlet* was one of Shakespeare's most popular plays when it was first produced, and it has continued to be the most well known and frequently performed of Shakespeare's plays in the four hundred years since his death. His work has appeared in just about every medium imaginable: from radio and television to ballet, opera, and even comic books. Some of his most memorable lines and verses, such as "To be or not to be …" from *Hamlet*, have become common phrases in the English language. Hamlet has even appeared as a character on *The Simpsons*, the long-running animated sitcom.

Perhaps Shakespeare is so timeless because he is closer to our hearts than other literary greats. Throughout history, audiences have found that his comedies and tragedies relate to humanity's ageless questions. Reading Shakespeare

This portrait from around 1610 depicts a middle-aged Shakespeare.

The Shakespeare Globe Theatre in London, England

allows us to understand not only the world we inhabit, but also ourselves.

As few records were kept in Shakespeare's day, we know only sketchy details about his actual life. The exact date of his birth is unknown, but he was born in the town of Stratford-upon-Avon, Warwickshire, England on or about April of 1564. In 1582, when he was eighteen years old, he married Anne Hathaway. Their first child was born six months later. Twins arrived the following year. By the early 1590s Shakespeare was a member of London's leading acting company, the Lord Chamberlain's Men. The company's star actor, Richard Burbage, played many of Shakespeare's greatest roles.

William owned a share in the company. This gave him the opportunity to build his own theater. The Globe was erected in 1599 on the banks of the Thames River. After the death of Queen Elizabeth I, the new king, James I, awarded the acting company a royal patent. They changed their name to the King's Men. People from all backgrounds came to the Globe to see the King's Men perform. They were attracted to the Bard's plays for the same reasons we are today: they addressed the age-old questions with which humanity has always struggled. What's more, Shakespeare's writing—peppered with jokes, insults, and contemporary references—was accessible and understandable even to those from lowborn backgrounds. Even in the twenty-first century, Shakespeare's plays continue to attract a diverse audience.

The exact date of Shakespeare's death is debated, but he was buried in the Holy Trinity Church on April 25, 1616. The epitaph carved into his tombstone contains a warning to those who would move him:

> ***Blessed be the man that spares these stones,***
> ***And cursed be he that moves my bones.***

It's fitting that Shakespeare's work, much like his life, is subject to interpretation. Each new examination or adaptation reveals to us something surprising.

Chapter One

Shakespeare and *Hamlet*

The Tragedy of Hamlet, Prince of Denmark, usually dated around 1600, has been the subject of thousands of books and articles. The sometimes violent but supremely eloquent character of Hamlet himself is one of the most challenging roles ever written for any actor.

Hamlet originates from an obscure, and very crude, legend of a Danish prince avenging his father, who was murdered by his uncle. The uncle marries the prince's mother and becomes king. Shakespeare sets his play in the sixteenth century of the Christian era, during the time of the Reformation. Prior to reading the play, it might be useful to have a basic knowledge of the Bible and of Catholic and Protestant views on matters such as the sacraments and purgatory.

Most scholars date Shakespeare's tragedy to about 1600; they explain references to a *Hamlet* play in 1589, 1594, and 1596 by suggesting that there was an earlier

Ophelia and Laertes, William Gorman Wills's 1879 painting

play by that name. They have dubbed this play the *Ur-Hamlet* (or, the earliest version) and assume it was the immediate source of Shakespeare's masterpiece. But this is sheer speculation; no positive evidence proves that such a play ever existed. No author was named and no text of it has survived. Still the idea of the play *Ur-Hamlet* has become dogma in Shakespearean scholarship.

Another curious fact deepens the mystery of *Hamlet*: we possess three distinct versions of the play's text. One is the very short "bad" quarto (or small individual edition) of 1603; another is the much longer "good" quarto of 1604; the third is the version published in the great folio of the plays in 1623, which is nearly identical to the "good" quarto. This third version deletes about two hundred lines from the 1604 copy and adds about seventy new ones. Most modern editions, including this one, combine the 1604 and 1623 texts.

The "bad" quarto appears to be an actor's botched attempt to reconstruct the play from memory; it is mostly a mess, comically making a mess of the play's most famous speeches. Hamlet's great soliloquy, for instance, begins like this: "To be, or not to be, aye, there's the point: / To die, to sleep; is that all? Aye, all. / No, to sleep, to dream, aye, marry there it goes …"

The "bad" quarto does tell us that the play was very popular by 1603 and had been widely performed in London, at the universities at Oxford and Cambridge, "and elsewhere."

Chapter Two

The Play's the Thing

Act I, Scene 1

Overview

It is a bitterly cold midnight on the ramparts of the king's castle at Elsinore in Denmark. The sentinel Francisco is relieved by another, Barnardo. Marcellus is coming, too, and he will bring with him the scholar Horatio, who does not believe what these men say—that they have seen on the previous two nights a sinister ghost that looks exactly like the dead King Hamlet. They hope Horatio will not only see the ghost but also get it to speak.

Suddenly the Ghost appears, wearing armor. Horatio orders it to speak to him, but when it seems about to, it says nothing and marches away as if offended.

After the Ghost has gone, the three men speculate on what its appearance may mean. Denmark is feverishly preparing for war with Norway. Horatio recalls that old King Hamlet had been dared to engage in single combat

This poster is from the 1948 film adaptation of *Hamlet*, starring Laurence Olivier.

by King Fortinbras of Norway, each wagering a certain amount of land on the outcome. Hamlet had won, slaying Fortinbras; now young Fortinbras, the dead king's son, has raised an army and seeks to recover the lands his father lost. (The name Fortinbras means "strong arm.") Horatio thinks this may somehow explain why the Ghost is appearing now.

During these speculations the Ghost returns. Again Horatio tells it to explain itself and it seems about to speak when the cock crows, whereupon it departs "like a guilty thing / Upon a fearful summons."

As dawn breaks, Marcellus mentions the legend that ghosts cannot appear to men during the Christmas season, when the nights are wholesome and fairies and witches are powerless. Horatio says he believes this "in part," and urges that they report the Ghost's appearance to young Prince Hamlet; surely it will speak to him! The others agree, and Marcellus knows where they will find Hamlet this morning.

Analysis

This scene is a masterpiece of drama and exposition. Within barely fifty lines Shakespeare creates terrific dramatic tension. The entire scene, in less than two hundred lines, takes us plausibly from midnight to dawn. Shakespeare manipulates our sense of time with astounding skill.

Throughout the scene the Ghost is ambiguous but menacing, "a guilty thing" that is "fair" yet "warlike" in form. It shuns the daylight. What can it mean?

> ***"It started like a guilty thing upon a fearful summons"***

Act I, Scene 2

Overview

As the day continues Denmark's new king, Claudius, is addressing his court at Elsinore. His brother Hamlet has recently died; he has married the widow, Queen Gertrude, and assumed the throne. He thanks the dignitaries for their support in these recent events.

Turning to foreign matters, he notes that young Fortinbras is threatening to invade Denmark with his army to regain those lands his father lost to the old King Hamlet. Claudius sends two diplomats, Cornelius and Voltimand, to Norway to ask the ailing old king to control his nephew.

Once they are gone, Claudius turns to young Laertes, son of his chief counselor, Polonius, to ask about a request he has mentioned. Laertes says he would like permission to return to Paris, from where he has come to witness Claudius's coronation. When Polonius nods his reluctant approval, the king grants his wish.

Kronborg Castle in Helsingør, Denmark, was the model for Elsinore in Hamlet.

Now Claudius turns to his nephew Hamlet, who is still wearing black, in mourning for his father. Claudius asks why Hamlet is taking his father's passing so hard; Hamlet answers with bitter sarcasm: "I am too much in the sun" (note the pun on "son").

Hamlet's mother, Gertrude, asks the same question, since death is every human being's common lot. When Hamlet agrees that death is "common," she asks why, then, it "seems" so "particular" with him. He retorts that it not only "seems," it really "is" ("I know not 'seems'"). The depth of his grief is far deeper than externals such as his "inky cloak" and his tears and sighs, "For they are actions that a man might play."

Professing love for Hamlet as his "son" and heir to the throne of Denmark, Claudius reminds Hamlet that every father dies eventually, and chides Hamlet for his prolonged grieving. He especially hopes Hamlet will not go back to school in Wittenberg. Claudius fears Hamlet and wants him to stay in Elsinore where he can watch him.

Hamlet ignores this appeal, but when Gertrude makes the same plea, he sulkily agrees. The king, queen, and other courtiers leave him alone, and he delivers his first great soliloquy: "O that this too too solid Flesh would melt …"

Hamlet is nearly suicidal; he wishes that God had not condemned "self-slaughter." He is distraught not only over his father's death, which he could have handled, but especially over his mother's hasty, incestuous marriage to a man he regards as contemptible: "My father's brother, but no more like my father / Than I to Hercules."

He is heartbroken, but his mood brightens as soon as he recognizes an old friend: his fellow student Horatio, accompanied by Marcellus and Barnardo. He asks why Horatio has come all the way from Wittenberg. Horatio replies: "My lord, I came to see your father's funeral." With the quick wit we have already seen, Hamlet retorts, "I pray thee, do not mock me, fellow-student; / I think it was to see my mother's wedding." True, Horatio admits; the marriage closely followed the funeral. It was "thrift," Hamlet quips; so that the meats baked for the funeral could serve as cold cuts for the marriage festivities.

When Hamlet recalls his father, Horatio gets to the point of his visit: "I think I saw him yesternight." He describes the Ghost and its effect on his terrified companions, who were "distilled / Almost to jelly with the act of fear." He is sure that the Ghost will come again tonight. Hamlet resolves to join them on the sentries' platform before midnight; and he will speak to the Ghost himself, no matter what the risk. He suspects that it is coming to speak of "foul play."

Analysis

Claudius is settling into his new role as king with finesse and aplomb. He suavely addresses several problems that confront him, asserting his authority with ease: first, his kingship itself, with his somewhat dubious marriage to his brother's widow; second, the threat from young Fortinbras of Norway; third, Laertes's eagerness to return to France; and finally, his disgruntled nephew Hamlet's prolonged mourning for his dead father (and his bitter rejection of Claudius's new order). Hamlet's first soliloquy reveals the depth of his discontent: it verges on the suicidal.

This scene once again displays Shakespeare's mastery of exposition. He conveys a remarkable amount of information with extreme economy, laying the groundwork for the whole tragedy. The university at Wittenberg, site of the new Protestant movement and much religious controversy, is mentioned four times within a few lines. The play never mentions it again, but this is enough to tell us (and a literate Elizabethan spectator) that Hamlet is aware of the great theological disputes of his day, toward which the play seems, on the surface at least, carefully noncommittal.

The suspense about the Ghost's meaning and purpose—and, in fact, its very nature—continues to build. Hamlet will get some answers when he speaks to it tonight—or so we hope.

Act I, Scene 3

Overview

Later that day Laertes is about to sail for France, but before he leaves he warns his sister Ophelia to beware of Hamlet, who, being a prince, may be free to compromise her sexually and ruin her honor. Even if Hamlet sincerely loves her now, he is young and may change his mind. Ophelia listens, but teases her brother by telling him that he had better behave himself in France and practice the virtues he preaches.

Polonius comes to say good-bye to his son, adding some "precepts" on wise behavior. He counsels thrift, moderation, prudence, and so forth.

Once Laertes is gone, Polonius also warns Ophelia against Hamlet. He is even more cynical than his son: Polonius thinks Hamlet's interest in Ophelia is purely sexual, and he bluntly orders her to have nothing more to do with Hamlet. She meekly promises to obey.

Analysis

Polonius's precepts to Laertes all sound sensible, but they show Polonius to be almost Hamlet's opposite: a man who

Ophelia, Polonius, and Laertes in the 1948 film version of *Hamlet*

prizes thrift, caution, and safety above everything else. He cares nothing for nobility of soul or other purely moral qualities. It is instructive to contrast his advice to Laertes with Hamlet's generous praise of Horatio in Act III, Scene 2.

He is even more narrow-minded in his orders to Ophelia. He is strict because he is suspicious; he has no faith in either his daughter or Hamlet. She, on the other hand, recognizes that Hamlet is "honorable" in his vows of love, and her father's command to avoid him crushes her spirit.

This scene also prepares us for what is to come. Polonius is a tyrannical father and a windbag. Later he will be Hamlet's antagonist, far out of his depth with both the prince and the king. His limitations will prove disastrous for himself and others.

"Neither a borrower nor a lender be"

Act I, Scene 4

Overview

As agreed, Hamlet meets Horatio and Marcellus on the sentries' platform near midnight the same day to await the Ghost. They hear the sound of drums and cannons in the castle below. Hamlet explains that the king is up late carousing, and these noises accompany his drinking and revelry. This is an old Danish custom, he says, "a custom / More honored in the breach than in the observance," since it has given the Danes a reputation for drunkenness, obscuring their real virtues. The same is true of individuals, he reflects: a single vice may blind the world to all their good qualities.

These thoughts are interrupted by the appearance of the Ghost. Hamlet immediately speaks to it. Unsure whether it is "a spirit of health" or a "goblin damned," he greets it as his father and begs it to say something to him.

When the Ghost beckons Hamlet to follow, Horatio and Marcellus warn Hamlet not to go. The Ghost may lead him over a cliff or draw him into madness; who knows what it may do? But Hamlet insists on following it, saying:

Horatio attempts to hold Hamlet back from confronting the Ghost.

> ***I do not set my life at a pin's fee;***
> ***And for my soul, what can it do to that,***
> ***Being a thing immortal as itself?***

When Horatio and Marcellus try to hold Hamlet back, Hamlet orders them to let go, or he will "make a ghost" of whoever lays hands on him. (Even in moments of danger, Hamlet's wit never deserts him.)

The two men, fearing for Hamlet, follow at a distance. Marcellus says darkly, "Something is rotten in the state of Denmark." But Horatio has faith, saying, "Heaven will direct it." Marcellus is not so sure.

Analysis

The first time we see Hamlet presented with a crisis, he shows courage, purpose, and presence of mind. He is a commanding personality. The defiance he showed Claudius earlier was similar to his instant readiness to confront the dreadful ghost, even if it is a "goblin damned." His friends fear that he may be *too* courageous, considering the dangers they apprehend. But as he says, "My fate cries out."

Later Hamlet will accuse himself of cowardice, but surely that is never his problem, except in his own imagination. Whatever Hamlet's flaws, timidity is not one of them. He is bold to a fault.

The Ghost has not yet revealed its true nature, but up to this point, it has been a foreboding figure, appearing only at night and seeming "warlike," "guilty," and terrifying.

Act I, Scene 5

Overview

Immediately thereafter, at another spot on the castle walls, Hamlet tells the Ghost to stop and speak; he refuses to follow it any farther. It tells him that it must soon give itself up to "sulphurous and tormenting flames." When Hamlet commiserates, "Alas, poor ghost!" it replies sternly, "Pity me not." And it demands revenge:

> *I am thy father's spirit,*
> *Doomed for a certain term to walk the night,*
> *And for the day confined to fast in fires,*
> *Till the foul crimes done in my days of nature*
> *Are burnt and purged away.*

It says that a full description of its sufferings would freeze Hamlet's blood and make his hair stand on end. Then it asks Hamlet, through his love as a son, to "Revenge [my] foul and most unnatural murder."

Hamlet cries:

Haste me to know't, that I, with wings as swift
As meditation or the thoughts of love,
May sweep to my revenge.

The story Claudius told was that old Hamlet was killed by a poisonous serpent as he slept in his orchard. But the truth, says the Ghost, is that "The serpent that did sting thy father's life / Now wears his crown."

Claudius is the murderer! "O my prophetic soul!" cries Hamlet. "My uncle!"

Yes, the Ghost explains: Claudius seduced Gertrude, then poured poison into King Hamlet's ears one afternoon, killing him before he could receive the sacrament of last rites to remove any sin from his soul. He died "With all my imperfections on my head. / O horrible! O horrible! Most horrible!" But in demanding revenge on Claudius, the Ghost orders Hamlet to spare Gertrude:

Leave her to heaven,
And to those thorns that in her bosom lodge
To prick and sting her.

The Ghost returns to the underworld with the parting command: "Remember me," although it is not likely that Hamlet will forget him.

"Remember thee!" sobs Hamlet. He promises to "wipe away" from his memory

> ***all trivial fond records,***
> ***All saws of books, all forms, all pressures past,***
> ***That youth and observation copied there,***
> ***And thy commandment all alone shall live***
> ***Within the book and volume of my brain,***
> ***Unmixed with baser matter.***

Horatio and Marcellus find Hamlet hysterical, not making much sense. He does not reveal what the Ghost has told him, ordering them: "Never make known what you have seen tonight." He insists that they swear by his sword. After they take the oath, the Ghost, under the earth, continues to cry out three times: "Swear."

Hamlet stipulates that they must never even hint that they know why he is behaving strangely, because in the future he may, he says, adopt an "antic disposition" for his own reasons. The two men accept all his conditions. As they part company Hamlet laments:

> ***The time is out of joint. O cursed spite,***
> ***That ever I was born to set it right!***

Analysis

The Ghost's words imply that it is being temporarily punished in purgatory, not eternally in hell. But many commentators have questioned this, for good reason. Christianity condemns revenge as a grave sin. And, as we will see later, Hamlet himself thinks that true revenge would mean killing Claudius while he is guilty of some mortal sin, sending him to hell forever.

Hamlet at first accepts revenge eagerly and uncritically as his duty. He promises that the Ghost's command will exist "all alone" in his mind and memory. But of course that would mean a serious loss of proportion, sacrificing everything he has ever learned in favor of one obsessive purpose. He is incapable of being so imbalanced, and it is to his credit that this is so. By the end of the scene the supposed duty of revenge has already become an unbearable burden to him.

Act II, Scene 1

Overview

Polonius is sending his servant Reynaldo (who appears only in this scene and is not heard of again) to take notes and money to Laertes in Paris. He also wants Reynaldo to do some spying. He suggests that one way to elicit gossip about Laertes might be to lay "slight sullies" on him—to speak of his minor vices, such as gambling, drinking, swearing, or even "drabbing" (going to prostitutes). Reynaldo is shocked, saying, "My lord, that would dishonor him!" But Polonius thinks it will not, if done tactfully. As he often does, he becomes so tangled in his own words that he forgets what he was about to say.

After Reynaldo leaves, Ophelia rushes into the room, frightened. She explains that Hamlet is behaving very oddly, bursting into her chamber unannounced and staring wordlessly at her, then, with a long sigh, walking backward out the way he came. It is apparent that some time has passed, allowing for Hamlet to set his strategy in motion.

Polonius decides that Hamlet has gone mad out of love after Ophelia rejected him. He admits that he misjudged

Hamlet, Horatio, and Marcellus encounter the late King Hamlet's ghost.

"By indirections, find directions out"

Hamlet when he warned Ophelia against him. But he feels he must tell the king about this.

Analysis

Polonius is revealed as an inveterate spy who respects nobody's privacy, least of all his own daughter's. This scene prepares us for his later snooping on Hamlet.

Ophelia reveals the weakness of her character, unable to stand up to her meddling father. We are not quite sure how to take her report of Hamlet's peculiar conduct. Is he pretending to be insane and trying to fool her, or is he testing her in the hope of being able to confide in her?

Act II, Scene 2

Overview

In this, the longest scene of the play (nine different characters appear in it), the mystery of the Ghost in the first act gradually becomes the broader mystery of human existence, as the characters try to figure one another out.

As the scene begins, Claudius and Gertrude welcome two of Hamlet's old friends, Rosencrantz and Guildenstern, to court. They have been "brought up" with him, and Claudius hopes they can discover the cause of Hamlet's "transformation," since neither "the exterior nor the inward man" of Hamlet's character is what it was before.

As the friends depart, Polonius arrives with good news. First, the ambassadors to Norway have returned after a successful mission. More important, Polonius thinks he has found "the very cause of Hamlet's lunacy."

Laurence Olivier depicts Hamlet in the 1948 film production.

Voltimand and Cornelius report that the old king of Norway has been grieved to learn of his nephew Fortinbras's attempt to invade Denmark and has ordered Fortinbras to stop, paying him a handsome amount to take his army to attack Poland instead, passing peacefully through Denmark. Claudius is satisfied with this arrangement and thanks the two diplomats for their troubles.

For some reason Claudius is more concerned with his nephew's strange behavior than with any foreign danger, and Polonius begins his wordy explanation of his belief that Ophelia's rejection of Hamlet has driven him mad. (He lies about why she rejected him, saying that he merely told her that Hamlet's high social rank as a prince ruled him out as a potential husband for her; he says nothing about his real and more cynical reason: that he was suspicious of Hamlet's motives.) He reads aloud a love letter that he says Hamlet wrote to Ophelia, and adds that Hamlet has undergone a decline from depression at her rejection to his present madness. This, at least, is Polonius's theory.

Claudius, not quite persuaded, wants to test Polonius's theory further. Polonius notes that Hamlet often walks for hours "here in the lobby" and proposes that they watch him from behind an "arras" (curtain) when Hamlet thinks he is alone with Ophelia. Claudius agrees.

Just then Hamlet arrives, reading a book. Claudius and Gertrude leave Polonius with him.

Adopting his "antic disposition," Hamlet teases the old man with disguised witticisms about various subjects, including his daughter. Thinking Hamlet is truly mad, Polonius takes him seriously, but notices that he sometimes makes a strange kind of sense. He never suspects that Hamlet is making a fool of him.

This goes on until Polonius leaves and Rosencrantz and Guildenstern return. Hamlet is delighted to see his old friends and drops the pretense of madness.

They exchange mildly bawdy jokes until Hamlet asks them why fortune has sent them "to prison hither," because "Denmark's a prison."

After a little more conversation, Hamlet forces Rosencrantz and Guildenstern to admit that they have come to Denmark because the king and queen have sent for them. He then admits that he has been in poor spirits lately, though he says he can give no reason for it; he has lost his mirth, ceased taking exercise, and suffered a general disillusionment with man and the whole world. Man, who is "the beauty of the world, the paragon of animals," now seems to him "the quintessence of dust."

"What a piece of work is man!"

Rosencrantz tries to cheer Hamlet up by telling him that his favorite company of actors is coming to the court; Rosencrantz and Guildenstern have met them on the way. Hamlet is elated when the actors, also old friends of his, arrive at court. Polonius now reenters to announce what Hamlet already knows: the actors are coming. Hamlet resumes baiting him about his daughter.

Hamlet greets the actors with real warmth, asking their star to recite one of Hamlet's favorite speeches, about the Trojan War, the slaughter of King Priam, and the grief of Queen Hecuba. The actor does so, breaking into tears as he delivers it.

Polonius is disgusted by this display of emotion, but Hamlet is moved and impressed. He orders Polonius to see that the actors are well taken care of. There will be a play at court tomorrow night.

Then he takes the leading actor aside and asks if the company can perform *The Murder of Gonzago*. The actor says yes. Hamlet then tells him that he will write a speech to be inserted into the play.

When he is alone, Hamlet delivers by far the longest of his soliloquies, beginning, "O what a rogue and peasant slave am I!" Most of it is violent self-reproach for his failure to keep the Ghost's command by killing Claudius.

Yet in the last few lines it takes a sudden turn. Hamlet—illogically, it seems—supposes that "the spirit that I have seen may be the devil" assuming his father's "shape" in order to "damn me" by provoking him to kill Claudius without justification. But the play to be presented tomorrow night will solve any mystery: if Claudius is guilty, his expression will show it when he sees his (alleged) crime reenacted on the stage. Hamlet ends the long speech with the cry

The play's the thing
Wherein I'll catch the conscience of the king!

Analysis

This episodic scene seems to cover a long period of time. With the scene before it, which indicates that Laertes has been in Paris for a while, it gives us the impression that months have elapsed. Likewise the return of the two ambassadors from Norway implies some passage of time. Shakespeare manipulates our sense of time with admirable subtlety.

This is quite a change of pace from the first act, which covered less than two days. This leisurely unfolding of events dissipates the dramatic fury of the early scenes. Polonius's fussy wordiness as he relates his opinions increases our feeling that time is now passing slowly. As Hamlet baits him, as Rosencrantz and Guildenstern try to help the king and queen find the cause of Hamlet's odd behavior, as the actors come to Elsinore and prepare for the play, we nearly forget about the Ghost and the murder of Hamlet's father.

Hamlet attempts to make Guildenstern play the recorder.

Then suddenly Hamlet's final soliloquy reminds us. He savagely upbraids (scolds) himself for his delay in killing Claudius, contrasting his own lack of emotion over his father's murder with the artificial passion of the actor over the grief of Hecuba.

Hamlet says he is "prompted to my revenge by heaven and hell," but then says—for the first time, without any advance notice, at the very end of the scene—that "the spirit that I have seen may be the devil" impersonating his father's spirit.

This is a stunning development. After listening to the Ghost, Hamlet had assured Horatio and Marcellus that it was "an honest ghost." Now, some time later, he suggests the very opposite. And he has decided to use the device of a play, recreating the alleged crime in front of Claudius, to test the Ghost's word.

Why has he come to doubt what he had been so sure of? Why is he calling his duty into question: The promise he made to "sweep" when he told the Ghost he would keep its command "all alone" in his memory?

Act III, Scene 1

Overview

As Hamlet lays a trap for Claudius, Claudius and Polonius lay one for Hamlet.

Claudius questions Rosencrantz and Guildenstern about what they have managed to learn from Hamlet of the reason for his "transformation." They can report little except frustration; he received them "most like a gentleman," but volunteered no helpful information, except that he was adopting "a crafty madness."

But Claudius is pleased to learn that Hamlet's spirits are so good that he plans to stage a play for the court this very night, inviting the king to attend. Claudius, suspecting nothing beyond innocent amusement, agrees to come.

Meanwhile, he and Polonius will hide behind a curtain to observe Hamlet with Ophelia. Polonius tells his daughter to read a religious book to create an impression of piety. He remarks regretfully on the hypocrisy of feigning religious appearances, and Claudius says, in an aside to the audience, that Polonius's remark stings his own bad conscience.

"To be or not to be:
that is the question"

Shakespeare in the Movies

WE KNOW THAT Shakespeare's stories continued to resonate long after his life. So is it any wonder that throughout the last century, several films have appeared that are actually adaptations of Shakespeare scripts in disguise?

There aren't any singing animals in *Hamlet*, but after reading or watching Disney's *The Lion King*, the parallels cannot be ignored. A brother kills a king so that he can take the throne. A ghost appears to the young prince, ordering him to claim his destiny. Two friends accompany the king's son, Simba, and serve as comic relief; could Timon and Pumbaa be "Disneyfied" versions of Rosencrantz and Guildenstern?

Shakespeare's plays have also been adapted into teenage romantic comedies. In the late 1990s, *10 Things I Hate About You* modernized *The Taming of the Shrew*. Just like in the play, a father decides that before his younger daughter can do something, the older daughter has to do it first. In the play, the youngest daughter is forbidden from marriage, but in the movie the dad merely prohibits dating, boys, and attending dances. Both the heroine of the movie and her bad boy love interest are based on the play's lead characters.

More recently, *She's the Man* borrowed the names of *Twelfth Night*'s characters, its jokes, and even its most famous line: "Be not afraid of

Disney's *The Lion King* takes many of its narrative cues from Hamlet.

greatness. Some are born great, some achieve greatness, and others have greatness thrust upon them." In 2013, *Warm Bodies* depicted a love affair not between two people from rival houses, but rather, a human and a zombie. That doomed romance is about as *Romeo and Juliet* as it can get. Fortunately, this one has a happier ending than the most famous tragedy of all time.

What do you think Shakespeare would say if he could see the movies that have been forged out of his plays?

Hamlet and Ophelia in the 1996 film adaptation, starring Kenneth Branagh and Kate Winslet

This is our first hint of what Hamlet will learn of the king's guilt. Claudius, by his own admission, is hiding something.

Claudius and Polonius conceal themselves as Gertrude, Rosencrantz, and Guildenstern depart and Hamlet comes in alone, delivering his most famous soliloquy, the one that begins with "To be or not to be." He compares death to a sleep in which we don't know whether we will dream, and to an "undiscovered country from whose bourn [boundary] no traveler returns." He is thinking of suicide, if death means an end of "the thousand natural shocks that flesh is heir to." But what if something worse follows after death? "Ay, there's the rub." This is why we finally decide to endure life after all: "Thus conscience does make cowards of us all." And in the end we may change all our great plans and do nothing.

Then he sees Ophelia and asks her prayers for "all my sins." She tells him that she wants to return the gifts—"remembrances"—he has given her. The word seems to ignite his fury; we recall his bitter memories of his mother ("Must I remember?") and his fervent vow to "remember" the Ghost.

Hamlet denies having given Ophelia anything and flies into a rage that she cannot comprehend. "Get thee to a nunnery," he tells her; "why wouldst thou be a breeder of sinners?" He is no worse than most men, he says, "yet it were better my mother had not borne me."

Suddenly suspicious, he asks where her father is. Her lie—"at home"—only makes his anger more violent. He rails against her, her father, all women, and marriage, then leaves her by herself. The distraught Ophelia is now certain that he is insane.

Claudius and Polonius emerge from behind the curtain. The king now thinks Hamlet's passion has nothing to do with rejected love; he knows the prince is sane. Polonius offers his usual advice: to eavesdrop. After the play he will hide and listen to what Gertrude says to her son. If her scolding fails to correct him, he can be sent to England or put into confinement. Claudius agrees.

Analysis

Now we are being prepared for the climactic confirmation of Claudius's guilt in the play scene. But there is no real mystery about it. Shakespeare tips us off by having Claudius reveal his bad conscience in a brief aside about his hypocrisy. Hamlet may be unsure of his uncle's guilt, but we are not.

Hamlet enters, deep in thought about whether it is nobler to suffer the outrages of fortune or to fight back. Is death really the end? It is the "undiscovered country" no traveler returns from—unless, of course, the problematic Ghost is such a traveler. But we cannot know, so we resign ourselves to the many evils we know in this life, made "cowards" by conscience and giving up on courageous action.

Noticing Ophelia, Hamlet breaks off thinking and questions her, not knowing that her father and Claudius are watching but nonetheless deeply suspicious of her. He turns on her all the anger that he has stored up against his mother; in his mind, all men are sinners and all women are seductresses.

Hearing Hamlet's explosion against women and marriage, Claudius realizes that whatever is preoccupying Hamlet, he is neither lovesick nor crazy; something must be done about him.

Act III, Scene 2

Overview

The fateful night commences. The play, *The Murder of Gonzago*, is about to begin. Hamlet advises the actors on how to deliver their lines, stressing the need for natural-seeming moderation and warning against overacting but

Edwin Austen Abbey's 1897 painting depicts the play scene from *Hamlet*.

also against being "too tame." He also urges that the clowns not be allowed to improvise or to add lines not in the script. Passion must be kept under control.

"To hold, as 'twere, the mirror up to nature"

Now Hamlet turns to his friend Horatio, praising him with deep warmth for his self-control, his superiority to the whims and vicissitudes of fortune, for not being "passion's slave." The fiery, volatile Hamlet recognizes that Horatio, steadily calm and rational, is, temperamentally, both his opposite and his superior. In short, Horatio is the soul of reason.

Returning to the immediate situation, Hamlet tells Horatio that the play will reenact what the Ghost has confided to him about King Hamlet's murder. If Claudius's reaction to the scene fails to expose "his occulted guilt," then "it is a damned ghost that we have seen." Horatio agrees to observe Claudius closely.

They join the courtiers to watch the play. Forgetting all his own counsel against being controlled by passion, Hamlet baits everyone with sarcasm—Polonius, Claudius, Gertrude, and, most obscenely, Ophelia.

The play begins with a dumb show, or wordless pantomime, showing the murder. Hamlet, vexed, expresses irritation. The actors perform the story again, this time aloud, according to the script Hamlet has written himself. It is designed to implicate Gertrude, whom Hamlet suspects of complicity in the murder, but Gertrude fails to perceive this.

He continues to comment freely as the play proceeds, the actor playing the queen falsely promises to be faithful to her husband's memory if he dies. Hamlet is sure this "wormwood" must be galling to her, but Gertrude still fails to see any parallel to herself. Hamlet asks how she likes the play; she answers obtusely, "The lady doth protest too much, methinks."

Claudius, however, has begun to suspect something. He asks Hamlet if there is any "offense" in the story. Not at all, Hamlet says merrily: "Your majesty, and we that have free souls, it touches us not."

At last the actor playing the murderer makes his entrance with the poison he intends to use to kill the actor playing the king. Hamlet identifies him as "Lucianus, nephew to the king." As he pours the poison into his victim's ear, Hamlet cries: "He poisons him i'th' garden for his estate. … You shall see anon how the murderer gets the love of Gonzago's wife."

These impulsive comments confuse the courtiers, who think Hamlet, a nephew, is somehow threatening to kill Claudius. But Claudius himself grasps the point: Hamlet knows about his crime!

Claudius rises, calling for light. The play breaks up. The courtiers depart with the king, leaving Hamlet and Horatio by themselves.

Hamlet is elated, triumphant. He has learned what he wanted to know. His hated uncle is guilty! "O good Horatio, I'll take the Ghost's word for a thousand pound. Didst perceive? … Upon the talk of the poisoning?"

Yes, Horatio has seen it all, but is more subdued. He realizes that Hamlet, carried away by emotion, has misplayed his opportunity. His apparent victory will bring new dangers.

Rosencrantz and Guildenstern enter. Hamlet calls for recorder music to celebrate. His old friends tell him that Claudius and Gertrude are very upset with him, and that the queen wants to see him in her chamber. Hamlet replies with gloating sarcasm; he now regards these old friends as contemptible enemies.

They are still baffled by his behavior. He says the reason for the way he is acting is that he lacks "advancement." But, says Rosencrantz, the king himself has already announced that Hamlet will succeed him! Hamlet replies by partially citing the old proverb: "While the grass grows, the horse starves." He does not intend to wait for Claudius to die.

He challenges Guildenstern to play the recorder; when Guildenstern replies that he cannot, Hamlet unloads further sarcasm on him: "You would play upon me … [D]o you think that I am easier to be played on than a pipe?"

Polonius arrives and tells Hamlet again that Gertrude wants to speak with him at once. Hamlet teases the old man again, but he agrees to see his mother.

Left alone, Hamlet reflects that this is the witching hour, and he feels ready to "drink hot blood": he must not yield to "the soul of Nero" and kill his own mother. He is tempted to kill her, not Claudius.

Analysis

In two speeches, first to the actors and then to Horatio, Hamlet discourses on the virtue of keeping passion under control. But throughout the scene his own passions get the better of him. He taunts everyone at court and all but ruins the play he has so carefully planned.

He cannot shake his baseless suspicion that his mother has helped Claudius murder his father. He writes this into the script of *The Murder of Gonzago* to test her reaction, then fails to notice when she seems to be quite innocent.

That script repeats the theme of passion:

> ***What to ourselves in passion we propose,***
> ***The passion ending, doth the purpose lose.***
>
> ***Our wills and fates do so contrary run***
> ***That our devices still are overthrown;***
> ***Our thoughts are ours, their ends none***
> ***of our own.***

These passages serve as good comments on Hamlet himself.

Hamlet thinks the play device has succeeded when Claudius reveals his guilt to Hamlet and Horatio, but the other courtiers, disturbed by Hamlet's "antic" behavior, never perceive that Claudius is guilty. They just think their belief that the prince is deranged or irresponsible is confirmed.

After Claudius interrupts the play, Hamlet rashly assumes that he has won the battle of wits. Horatio, always more solemn, knows better.

The entrance of Rosencrantz and Guildenstern proves that Horatio is correct. They give no indication of realizing the true meaning of Claudius's behavior; it is Hamlet's behavior that concerns and baffles them. Likewise, Polonius sees only that Hamlet is still acting wildly.

In his soliloquy ending the scene, Hamlet reveals that his passion is still dangerously out of his own control: he fears he may kill not his uncle, but his mother.

Act III, Scene 3

Overview

Claudius orders Rosencrantz and Guildenstern to prepare to escort Hamlet to England. He is too dangerous to be permitted to stay in Denmark. They agree, of course, having missed the whole point of Claudius's own explosion at the play.

Polonius, wordy as always, tells Claudius that Hamlet is on his way to Gertrude's chamber, where Polonius himself will be hiding to overhear whatever is said.

Now Claudius is alone, and he delivers his own long soliloquy. He is sick with guilt at his crime, the crime of Cain in the Bible, "a brother's murder." He is torn. He wants to repent, but he cannot bear to give up the fruits of his crime: "my crown, mine own ambition, and my queen." In this world, he reflects, a man can have it both ways, but not in heaven. He falls to his knees, trying to pray.

As he kneels, Hamlet comes by and, seeing his chance for revenge, draws his sword: "Now might I do it pat, now he is praying." But he immediately reasons that if he kills Claudius at prayer, the king may go straight to heaven! "Why, this is hire and salary, not revenge." After all, Claudius killed Hamlet's father "grossly," "with all his crimes broad-blown, as flush as May," so why should Hamlet kill him in "the purging of his soul / When he is fit and season'd for his passage?"

Sheathing his sword, Hamlet decides to delay his revenge until he can catch his uncle committing a sin, perhaps "in the incestuous pleasure of his bed," so that "his soul may be as damn'd and black as hell, whereto it goes."

But as soon as Hamlet has gone, Claudius rises. He has been unable to pray sincerely. He realizes that he has chosen damnation after all.

Analysis

This scene makes it clear that Hamlet knows that his father's ghost has come from hell, not purgatory. He has died without the sacraments in the midst of his "crimes"—"foul crimes," as he called them.

The eighteenth-century English literary critic Samuel Johnson called Hamlet's soliloquy "too horrible to be read or uttered," because the prince is not content with mere justice—blood for blood—but actually seeks to damn his enemy's soul, which is itself a damnable sin.

Fierce as this may sound, Hamlet still seems less angry at his uncle than at his mother.

Act III, Scene 4

Overview

In Gertrude's chamber Polonius urges the queen to scold her son severely for his "pranks." The old man still cannot comprehend the real gravity of the situation. He hides behind a hanging tapestry as Hamlet approaches.

When Hamlet arrives Gertrude accuses him: "Hamlet, thou hast thy father much offended"—meaning Claudius. He retorts, "Mother, you have my father much offended"—meaning that she has murdered his real father. Seeing his fury, she thinks he is about to kill her and calls for help.

Hamlet in Gertrude's chamber

Polonius calls for help, too. Hearing the voice, Hamlet stabs through the tapestry, thinking it is Claudius. He lifts the tapestry and finds that he has killed Polonius.

When Gertrude calls this "a rash and bloody deed," Hamlet retorts: "A bloody deed! Almost as bad, good mother, / As kill a king and marry with his brother." She gasps, "As kill a king?" Suddenly he realizes that she is innocent of his father's murder. He hurls abuse at Polonius's corpse: "Thou wretched, rash, intruding fool, farewell. / I took thee for thy better."

Analysis

Hamlet here turns the tables on himself. He first had the inspired thought of exposing his uncle's guilt by staging a play reenacting the murder of his father, but he partly wasted the opportunity by letting his passions get the better of him, despite his own wise words to both the actors and Horatio about self-control. Therefore, everyone at court except Claudius (and Horatio) missed the point, thinking Hamlet was insanely threatening the king.

Now, in his anger at Gertrude's sins, his passions betray him again: he draws his sword on her, frightening her so badly that she calls for help. When Polonius, hiding behind the tapestry, joins her cry, Hamlet impulsively stabs him, mistaking him for Claudius. This killing puts him in his enemy's power. He has lost the advantage and initiative he enjoyed at the beginning of the evening. And he has also, as we see later, made another deadly enemy: Polonius's son, Laertes.

In his cooler moments, Hamlet has never really wanted to kill Claudius, much as he hates him. Now he turns his rage on his mother for her sins of lust. His fury at her is so violent that the Ghost appears to him (but remains invisible to Gertrude) to remind him that he is supposed to kill Claudius, not to vent his passion at his mother.

But it is too late. Hamlet is now being sent to England by Claudius's order. He has wasted his chance to put Claudius at his mercy, and now his own life is in grave danger.

Act IV, Scene 1

Overview

Claudius finds Gertrude in great agitation, tearful and sighing. He asks her what has upset her, but she, now suspicious of her husband, gives him a shaded account of events. Hamlet, in a mad moment, has mistaken Polonius for a rat and stabbed him to death. Thinking first of himself, as always, Claudius realizes that had he been there, he would have met the same fate. He calls Rosencrantz and Guildenstern and orders them to bring Hamlet and Polonius's body.

Analysis

Gertrude is now unsure what to think, but she instinctively tries to protect her son from her self-centered husband. Claudius's suave charm cannot conceal his essential cynicism.

Act IV, Scene 2

Overview

Hamlet teases Rosencrantz and Guildenstern about where he has stowed the body, turning it into a game of hide-and-seek. He also taunts them about their sycophantic obedience to the king.

Analysis

Hamlet despises his old schoolfellows for their lack of character. Unlike his only real friend, Horatio, they are amoral puppets of chance, willing to do whatever they are told.

Act IV, Scene 3

Overview

Rosencrantz and Guildenstern bring Hamlet to the king under guard. Ever the smooth hypocrite, Claudius feigns love for his nephew. But of course Hamlet is undeceived and replies, as always, with his own insolent wit. When Claudius tells Hamlet he must go to England—for his own good, of course—Hamlet fully realizes that he is going to be murdered there. After he is escorted away, Claudius, in a soliloquy, expresses his eagerness for his nephew's death in England, for which he has already sealed a written order. (England, in the story, is a territory under Denmark's control.)

Analysis

The enmity between Hamlet and Claudius is now all but open. Among the play's characters, only Rosencrantz and Guildenstern are still fooled, thinking that Claudius means well and that Hamlet is the sole troublemaker. Hamlet stings his uncle with some of his most piercing witticisms, such as when he explains how "a king may go a progress through the guts of a beggar."

Sir John Millais's 1852 depiction of Ophelia drowning

Act IV, Scene 4

Overview

Fortinbras of Norway arrives on Danish soil with his army. He plans to invade Poland and gives assurances that he has no hostile or aggressive intentions toward Denmark.

In his final soliloquy, Hamlet, who is on his way to England when he meets this army, once again expresses shame that he has delayed his revenge so long. He feels shamed by the courage of the Norwegians, who are ready to shed their blood over a mere patch of Polish territory, a plot of ground too small to bury the men who will die fighting for it.

Analysis

This short scene includes a soliloquy on revenge that tells us almost nothing beyond what we already knew. Hamlet, now under the control of others, has lost the ability to act on his intentions, making the soliloquy futile. There is some evidence that Shakespeare cut the speech in his final revision of the play.

Act IV, Scene 5

Overview

The content clues in this scene indicate the second long passage of time in the events of the play. Ophelia has gone mad. Her father is dead, killed by Hamlet, who has violently rejected her. Meanwhile her brother, Laertes, has been gone for months. She is friendless. She sings bits of old songs without making much sense, and she hands out flowers to everyone around her.

Gertrude is now guilt-stricken about her marriage. The sight of the raving Ophelia adds to her unease. Claudius comments on the multiplicity of sorrows.

Just when it seems as if things could hardly get worse, Laertes arrives home from France, leading a riotous mob that wants to make him their new king. He is enraged to hear of Polonius's death and demands to know how it happened so he can take revenge.

Claudius handles Laertes deftly, promising to give him justice and affirming his own innocence without saying anything to frighten Gertrude. Poor Ophelia enters, singing mad ballads, and Laertes's wrath is redoubled. All is going well for Claudius, it seems.

Analysis

Claudius's cool hypocrisy reaches its nadir, or lowest point, when he tells his attendants to let the furious Laertes go.

Hamlet is more forgiving of his uncle, Claudius, than he is of his mother, Gertrude.

The king is safe from any harm, he says, because God protects kings from treason.

Laertes has no qualms about revenge:

To hell, allegiance! Vows to the blackest devil!
Conscience and grace to the profoundest pit!
I dare damnation! To this point I stand,
That both the worlds I give to negligence,
Let come what comes; only I'll be revenged
Most thoroughly for my father.

He could hardly be more explicit than that. Unlike Hamlet, who says he is prompted to his revenge "by heaven and hell," Laertes takes a purely hellish view of it.

Revenge is satanic. This is the last word on the Ghost's fierce commandment to Hamlet.

Act IV, Scene 6

Overview

Horatio meets two sailors who bring him letters from Hamlet, one for him and some for the king and queen. Horatio reads that the sailors are pirates who overtook the ship that was taking Hamlet to England, captured him, and treated him well, knowing who he was. Now he owes them a good turn.

Hamlet says he will also tell Horatio other news when he sees him, particularly news about Rosencrantz and Guildenstern. Horatio tells the men to take him to Hamlet.

Analysis

This brief scene serves to tell us that Hamlet has never arrived in England and has come home. As always, he relies on Horatio.

Act IV, Scene 7

Overview

Having convinced Laertes that Hamlet was responsible for Polonius's death, Claudius is surprised to find out from Hamlet's letter that he is alive and back in Denmark. Claudius and Laertes plot Hamlet's death. They will use the king's favorite weapon: poison. They will stage a fencing match, and Laertes's rapier will have its tip treated with a venomous poison he has bought from a mountebank, or phony doctor. Hamlet will be too trusting to suspect mischief. But in case that fails, Claudius has a backup plan: poisoned wine for Hamlet to drink.

As they conspire, Gertrude brings shocking news: Ophelia has drowned, apparently a suicide. Laertes's hunger for revenge is intensified by this new grief.

Analysis

Emboldened by his successful crimes, Claudius is sure that his new plan to kill Hamlet is foolproof.

Act V, Scene 1

Overview

Two gravediggers, ignorant but sure of themselves, argue over the legalities of Ophelia's funeral. If she committed suicide, how can she be allowed a Christian burial? Somehow the coroner has ruled that she may. The two men agree that she is actually being allowed a regular funeral only because of her high social rank as a gentlewoman. It may be wrong, but this is the way the world works, and they can do nothing about it.

Hamlet and Horatio arrive at the graveyard, and Hamlet is slightly shocked and amused to hear one of the men singing as he digs a grave. (Horatio does not tell Hamlet for whom the grave is being dug. Either this is an oversight on Shakespeare's part or he assumes that the audience will not notice.)

As the gravedigger tosses old skulls out of the ground, Hamlet playfully wonders whose they may be. A politician's? A courtier's? A lord's? A lawyer's?

Hamlet questions the man about his grim trade, and the gravedigger answers with earthy humor, offering the prince a skull that once belonged to Yorick, the king's

Hamlet holds Yorick's skull in the 1996 film adaptation starring Kenneth Branagh.

jester. Hamlet is amazed. Taking the skull in his hand, he recalls that Yorick used to carry him on his back and kiss him when he was a small boy; now the memory disgusts him. He tells the skull to go to "my lady's chamber" and bid her apply her makeup an inch thick; she will end up looking just like this anyway.

"A ministering angel shall my sister be"

Hamlet keeps meditating and joking in this morbid vein, with Horatio mildly protesting that he is overdoing it, until he notices Claudius, Gertrude, Laertes, and the courtiers coming for the funeral. He is stunned when he realizes whose body they are following: Ophelia's.

Gertrude gently throws flowers on the corpse: "Sweets to the sweet." Laertes rages at the priest for denying Ophelia a full funeral service. The priest retorts that she would have been buried in unsanctified ground except that "great command"—meaning a special order from the king—had overruled the proper procedure.

Hamlet watches in horror as Laertes, wailing, leaps into the grave, hugs the corpse, and curses the man who caused her death. At this Hamlet steps forth and challenges Laertes, leaping into the grave to grapple with him. "The devil take thy soul!" Laertes cries. "Thou pray'st not well," quips Hamlet as Laertes tries to strangle him. Now everyone is yelling. Even Horatio tells Hamlet to calm down, saying, "Good my lord, be quiet!"

When peace is restored, Hamlet cannot understand Laertes's anger at him. Claudius counsels Laertes to be patient and follow their plan.

Analysis

This scene gives us one of the most emblematic moments in Western literature: Hamlet holding Yorick's skull. He confronts the mystery of death on the very day he himself is to die. This may be Shakespeare's most Shakespearean scene.

Yet again we see Hamlet's versatile wit in action as his mind plays on the many facets of dying and decay. He ranges from the law to ancient history to "my lady's chamber," generalizing philosophically without suspecting how imminent his own end is. He can meditate abstractly on death as the real men around him are scheming to kill him without his knowing it.

And, as usual, the sturdy Horatio seems to have more presence of mind. His head is never lost in the clouds. He is not at all puzzled as to why Laertes hates Hamlet.

The other characters live in the immediate moment, coping with their various practical problems. Hamlet acts as if he is going to live forever in the leisure of his own incomparable mind.

Act V, Scene 2

Overview

> *"There's a divinity that shapes our ends, Rough-hew them how we will"*

With this famous comment as prologue, Hamlet tells Horatio how he discovered, and defeated, Claudius's plan to have him murdered in England.

Unable to sleep on the ship one night, he opened the sealed letters and found the order that he should be beheaded as soon as he arrived. So, using his own familiarity with diplomatic language, he forged and substituted his own order: that Rosencrantz and Guildenstern should be put to death without even being allowed time for final confession.

Horatio is quietly shocked. He asks how this forged order was sealed. "Why, even in that was heaven ordinant," explains Hamlet. "I had my father's signet in my purse." This ring, for certifying official documents, enabled him to doom Rosencrantz and Guildenstern without the sacraments—just as his father had been doomed by Claudius.

When Horatio indicates quiet disapproval, Hamlet insists that "they are not near my conscience." After all,

The death of Hamlet in the 1913 film adaptation of the play

they asked for trouble by interfering in the battle of "mighty opposites," Hamlet and the king. Hamlet insists that it will also be "perfect conscience" to kill Claudius for his crimes and sins. And he adds that he now understands Laertes's outrage, since his cause—avenging a slain father—mirrors Hamlet's own.

At this point the courtier Osric approaches, making arrangements for the fencing match. Hamlet's mockery of Osric's precious manners goes over his head.

It is now time for the match. Hamlet has misgivings, but he dismisses Horatio's advice to heed them. He feels ready for anything, even death. He apologizes to Laertes, blaming his "madness" for Polonius's death, and Laertes pretends to accept this.

The match begins with Hamlet scoring two quick points. Gertrude, as a toast, drinks from the poisoned cup despite Claudius's attempt to stop her: "Gertrude, do not drink." When Hamlet fails to score a third point,

Laertes cheats during the pause and slightly wounds him with the rapier's poisoned tip. Hamlet, enraged, forces an exchange of rapiers and wounds Laertes. Gertrude falls. In a flash, Claudius's plot has unraveled: Hamlet, Laertes, and Gertrude are all about to die.

Gertrude cries that she has been poisoned. Hamlet, seeing "villainy," furiously calls for the door to be locked. Laertes realizes that all is lost and confesses: he and Hamlet are both poisoned. Gertrude is poisoned, too, and "the king's to blame."

Hamlet stabs Claudius with the poisoned rapier and pours some of the poisoned wine down his throat. As Claudius dies, Laertes begs Hamlet to "exchange forgiveness with me." Hamlet pardons him and says farewell to his dead mother.

Time has run out. Hamlet urgently orders Horatio to tell the whole story so that the world will understand his actions, sparing him "a wounded name"; Horatio wants to drink the poisoned wine, too, but Hamlet's dying anguish dissuades him.

Now Fortinbras arrives, freshly victorious from Poland. Hamlet predicts that he will be chosen Denmark's new king and endorses this result: "He has my dying voice." He breaks off in mid-sentence with his final words: "The rest is silence."

The English ambassador also arrives to tell Claudius that his order has been executed: Rosencrantz and Guildenstern are dead. The grieving Horatio tells both men that he will explain everything. Fortinbras orders that Hamlet, in death, be honored as a great warrior.

Analysis

Recounting his adventures to Horatio, Hamlet sees no irony in his having done to Rosencrantz and Guildenstern what Claudius did to old King Hamlet: consigned them to death without the sacraments. He says it was divine providence that enabled him to do this. It seems not to occur to him that both men were innocent. As far as they knew, they were simply serving their lawful monarch. They knew nothing of the murder that made him king or of his sealed orders for Hamlet's death.

Yet after this Hamlet appears to be at his happiest and most magnanimous. He sees Laertes's point of view and tries to make peace with him. He speaks to Claudius and Gertrude without spite or sarcasm. He is resigned to death, if that is God's will. This is a Hamlet we have hardly seen before.

And so Shakespeare's richest creation goes to his doom. His final thoughts are for the fate of Denmark and for his own reputation. Shakespeare never made a more remarkable character; only in *King Lear* would he imagine a more remarkable world.

List of Major Characters

- Hamlet, prince of Denmark
- Claudius, king of Denmark, uncle of Hamlet
- Ghost of King Hamlet, father of the prince
- Gertrude, queen of Denmark, Hamlet's widowed mother, now married to Claudius
- Polonius, counselor of Claudius
- Laertes, son of Polonius
- Ophelia, daughter of Polonius
- Horatio, friend and fellow student of Hamlet

Have We Found Shakespeare's Lost Play?

DUE TO THE scant nature of public records kept during the Elizabethan era, an aura of mystery surrounds William Shakespeare. We don't know where he went to school or his exact birthday. We also don't know if he wrote more than the thirty-seven plays commonly attributed to him. Two works, often called "the lost plays," are missing from Shakespeare's First Folio; this first published collection of his plays is considered the most reliable source for several of his works. Recently, researchers discovered that one of those plays might be *Double Falsehood*, a work that was published in 1728 and attributed to Lewis Theobald.

Double Falsehood, also called *The Distressed Lovers*, is based on a section of *Don Quixote*. It follows the exploits of two brothers, one who is good and the other sinful. Lewis Theobald had always claimed that he based the play off of three manuscripts written by Shakespeare, but scholars thought he was a fake. Now, new evidence indicates that it's very likely that Shakespeare wrote the play with assistance from his friend John Fletcher.

Researchers from the University of Texas at Austin used computer software to analyze thirty-three of Shakespeare's plays, nine of Fletcher's, and twelve of Theobald's. Through evaluating word

An edition of Shakespeare's First Folio dating from 1623

choices, phrase patterns, pronoun usage, and other factors, they created a "psychological signature" of each author, or a model of the writers' mental worlds. According to the researchers, the match between *Double Falsehood* and Shakespeare was a "landslide." Although Theobald had influenced the text, his impact was very minimal.

Without a doubt, skeptics will continue to question whether or not the play can truly be attributed to the Bard. Nevertheless, fans of Shakespeare will find it impossible to resist this gift of a lost—and found again—play.

Analysis of Major Characters

Hamlet

It has often been observed that Shakespeare put more of his own inexhaustible genius into Hamlet—poetic, superbly eloquent, witty, speculative, generous, cunning, imaginatively fertile, emotionally unpredictable—than into any other character. Hamlet is the only character we can imagine writing Shakespeare's plays. He towers above even the Bard's other greatest creations—the characters of Falstaff, Iago, and Cleopatra—though his rich personality also includes parts of each of them.

Beyond any doubt Hamlet is the most debated figure in world literature. Countless books have been written about him, as if he were a real historical figure. By some accounts, more books have been written about him than about any real men in history, except Jesus, Napoleon,

Władysław Czachórski's 1875 painting depicting Hamlet receiving the actors in court

Lincoln, and Hitler. Commentators have discussed at great length questions such as whether his madness is real or merely pretended, and why he delays his revenge so long. In the words of one critic, Shakespeare's characters seem so real because they are "as opaque as life's"; we can never quite have the last word about them. There is always more to be said, and this is especially true of Hamlet.

This fact is illustrated by the variety of interpretations he has received in the theater. Every actor wants to play this towering role, but no two actors play him in quite the same way, as can be seen by comparing the filmed versions of Laurence Olivier, Richard Burton, Nicol Williamson, Derek Jacobi, Mel Gibson, Kenneth Branagh, and Ethan Hawke. All of them have their virtues, but none is definitive. Some of them seem almost opposite: Olivier's fiery, athletic, heroic Hamlet could hardly be more unlike Branagh's light and whimsical prince, but who is to say that either is wrong? The character has room for all these readings, and many more.

Hamlet's wit is manifest from the first line he speaks: "A little more than kin, and less than kind." This at once sets him apart from the rest of the Danish court. Like most of Shakespeare's villains, oddly, he rejects the festivity of the society around him, but we soon learn that he is right to do so. Denmark is prematurely celebrating the arrival of a new king after the death of its old one. Its widowed queen has entered into a swift and scandalous marriage (an incestuous one, in fact) with her late husband's brother. The court's tolerance of this irregular union is a measure of its amorality.

Hamlet despises his uncle and makes no effort to hide his contempt, even before he learns of his father's murder.

Many actors and actresses have portrayed Hamlet, including Asta Nielsen in the 1920 German silent film.

He is sick with horror at his mother's behavior and wishes he could die. He longs to return to school at Wittenberg, where he can savor the quiet joys of a contemplative life, away from the corruption and strife of politics.

With his social inferiors, especially his fellow scholar Horatio, Hamlet is unfailingly gracious until he has reason to suspect them of betraying him to Claudius. He is shrewd enough to see through the scheming Polonius at once; his pure love for Ophelia is spoiled when she rejects him in obedience to her father and helps Polonius and Claudius spy on him. He warmly welcomes his old friends Rosencrantz and Guildenstern to court until he realizes that they, too, are working for his enemies.

"'Tis now the very witching time of night"

The arrival of the actors at Elsinore also delights him. They, at least, are his friends, and he sees how they can help him defeat the forces arrayed against him. For a few minutes he loses himself in a discussion of the art of acting, the essence of which, he explains, is "to hold, as't were, the mirror up to nature" by avoiding excesses of passion, clowning, and calling attention to oneself (good advice, which he himself forgets before the play has even begun). Hamlet's essential sweetness becomes clearest when he is alone with Horatio, before the play in Act III, before Ophelia's funeral in Act V, and again before the fatal fencing match with Laertes in the same act. Horatio is the only character with whom he is fully rational. (It is no accident that the name Horatio includes the Latin word for reason, *ratio*.)

Hamlet cherishes the memory of his dead father, whom he virtually worships. Compared to Claudius, he says, old Hamlet was Hyperion, the sun god, compared to a satyr, a lecherous figure of myth. He wonders how his mother could have preferred the miserable Claudius to such a man, whom he also likens to Hercules, Mercury, and Mars. (Significantly, the old man had "an eye like Mars"—the Roman god of war—"to threaten and command.") But all this excessive praise of his father makes the senior Hamlet sound more like a forbidding figure of awe than a loving, or lovable, husband and parent.

For most of the play Hamlet seems to hate Polonius even more than he hates Claudius, though the meddling old man is more foolish and annoying than wicked. It is true that Claudius has murdered his father and seduced and corrupted his mother; Polonius has merely deprived him of Ophelia (for surely he realizes, when she refuses to see him and sends back his letters, that this must be at her father's command).

Although Hamlet is extremely intelligent, he shows a curious blindness in one key respect. He idealizes his father and can see no redeeming virtues in Claudius. In fact, he can hardly bring himself to admit that Claudius is human. In this, he is seriously unrealistic. Time and again, Hamlet attributes to his father the qualities of pagan gods and heroes (but never, significantly, the Christian saints), whereas he persistently disparages his uncle as a satyr, a slave, a villain, a rat, a toad ("paddock"), a bat, a "cutpurse," a "bloat king," a tomcat ("gib"), and much more. The Ghost uses similar invectives, calling Claudius a "wretch" and "garbage" and himself "a radiant angel"—after admitting that he is consigned to suffer in fire for his own "foul crimes."

Hamlet's self-contradictions reach their lowest point when he actually fears that his (apparently praying) uncle may be repenting and going to heaven, while his father is being punished for dying "with all his crimes broad blown as flush as May." This is why Samuel Johnson and other Christian readers have been appalled by the speech beginning "Now might I do it pat."

"A hit, a very palpable hit"

Hamlet's unreasoning hatred of Claudius spills over into hostility toward anyone he perceives as an agent of the king, such as Polonius (and, by extension, Ophelia). He never stops to ask himself why people who know nothing of the Ghost and the murder should not try to serve and protect their king. To the court, it appears that Hamlet is making insanely wild and treasonous threats against a lawful monarch. Rosencrantz and Guildenstern argue reasonably that it is "most holy and religious fear" to defend the king (and Denmark as a whole) against such threats. For this reason they agree to escort Hamlet to England. They know of neither the murder of the old king nor of Claudius's secret order for Hamlet's murder; yet Hamlet calls these innocent men "adders fanged" and sends them to their death with his own forged order, callously remarking, "They are not near my conscience."

Many critics who see all the play's events only from Hamlet's perspective and share his obsession with Claudius's guilt fail to see that Hamlet is incurring some guilt of his own; his remark about the merry gravedigger who sings as he works applies to Hamlet, too: "The hand of little employment hath the daintier sense." We see his coarsening when, having killed Polonius, he quips cruelly, "I'll lug the guts into the neighbor room." He is at first unable to grasp why Laertes hates him and also blames him for Ophelia's madness and death. He has been corrupted, and morally blinded, by the Ghost's demand for revenge. Horatio and Marcellus were right to warn him against following that sinister figure.

To see Hamlet as an innocent and righteous avenger is to miss the point of the tragedy. He becomes part of

Denmark's rottenness and helps bring about its ruin. Claudius asks the furious Laertes,

> ***is't writ in your revenge***
> ***That, swoopstake, you will***
> ***draw both friend and foe,***
> ***Winner and loser?***

"None but his enemies," Laertes replies. But Claudius speaks more wisely than he knows: revenge by its nature is indiscriminate; it sweeps the innocent and the guilty together.

"Rosencrantz and Guildenstern are dead"

Hamlet's revenge will finally claim not only Claudius, but Hamlet himself, Gertrude (whom the Ghost ordered Hamlet to spare), and several others. In the end, the kingdom of Denmark itself falls in conquest to its old enemy, Norway. Can this be what the Ghost wanted when it made its first appearance in the story?

Maybe the play as a whole says to the Ghost, in effect, what the character of Portia says to another character, Shylock, in Shakespeare's *The Merchant of Venice*: "Thou shalt have justice—more than thou desirest." What is notably missing in the Denmark of *Hamlet* is mercy.

Claudius

The villain of *Hamlet*, the murderer of his own brother, is a brilliant, resourceful man, a worthy antagonist for his gifted nephew. Claudius is a smooth talker who knows

Hamlet's first attempt to take his revenge on Claudius

how to use power and handle people deftly. He proves that he is both shrewd and courageous. He is quick to sense danger from Hamlet and ruthless in protecting himself from every threat to his rule over Denmark.

Claudius sincerely loves Hamlet's mother, a still-attractive woman who is his equal in intelligence. He has married her to gain the Danish throne, but he clearly values her for her human qualities, too. Though he is not afraid of a fight, he is prudent enough to avoid conflict whenever possible. He quickly pacifies the outraged Laertes and, with marvelous tact, draws him into a conspiracy to murder Hamlet.

Although Claudius is supposedly his brother's opposite, he is not. If we listen to Hamlet and the Ghost, we are apt to mistake Claudius for a simple villain, when in fact he is anything but that. His conscience tortures him about the act he has committed, the crime of Cain, "a brother's murder." He could be the subject of his own separate tragedy, like *Macbeth*. In the end, his evil choices cancel out all his good qualities, which his nephew mercilessly refuses to acknowledge (even as he counts on Claudius's conscience to give away his guilt during the play, as indeed it does).

Hamlet and his father have their own sins to answer for. Almost the first thing the Ghost says is that he is being fearfully punished for his sins, a fact that hardly registers with Hamlet, who continues to idealize him and contrast him with Claudius anyway. Both common sense and religion (not to mention his own personal experience) should have warned Hamlet against imagining that two brothers could be as diametrically opposed as he imagines them to be.

Hate can breed wishful thinking as surely as love does. Hamlet *wants* his uncle to be as bad as possible.

Yet part of Claudius desperately wants to repent. After the play within the play we see him fall to his knees and try to pray. In his one long soliloquy (one that was deeply admired by Abraham Lincoln) he meditates as profoundly and passionately as Hamlet himself. What a terrible pity that these two men could not have been friends!

But Hamlet insists on idealizing his father and demonizing Claudius with equal unrealism. Far too many critics of the play have allowed themselves to be drawn into Hamlet's delusion that these brothers have nothing in common. From this, it is a short step to justifying Hamlet's supposed duty of revenge and missing the point of the tragedy.

"Alas, poor Yorick! I knew him, Horatio."

Ghost of King Hamlet

The Ghost is the spirit of hate, war, and violence. It appears in armor, "warlike," shrinks from the morning light, and appears "guilty." The shrewd and spiritually alert Horatio, who tries to induce it to talk, fears the worst: he tries to dissuade Hamlet from following it and speaking to it alone.

Whether it is, as Hamlet says, "an honest ghost"—telling the literal truth about Claudius's murder of his brother—is beside the point. As the character of Banquo says in another of Shakespeare's plays, *Macbeth*, hellish spirits may use even the truth to trick us into damning ourselves:

Oftentimes, to win us to our harm,
The instruments of darkness tell us truths,
Win us with honest trifles, to betray's
In deepest consequence.

If the Ghost's real purpose is to win Hamlet to his harm, damnation, then the accurate report of the murder in the orchard can be seen as an "honest trifle," and Hamlet is wasting his time trying to prove by experiment (testing Claudius's reaction to the play within the play) whether it is true. Hamlet commits a non sequitur (uses faulty logic) when he reasons that if the Ghost has told the truth about the crime, his revenge will be justified; but at first viewing or reading, we are apt to be swept along with him by our own passions, confusing angry revenge with impartial justice.

The mystery of the Ghost is never resolved for us; it remains an enigma. Is it distressed by the deaths of Hamlet and Gertrude and by the devastation of the Danish kingdom, or is all this ruin the fulfillment of its ultimate diabolical plan? Shakespeare leaves these questions unanswered, "Thoughts beyond the reaches of our souls."

"Frailty, thy name is woman"

Gertrude

Hamlet's mother has usually been regarded as a weak, stupid, passive woman. She is not. Her mind, like her son's, is quick and concise, going straight to the heart of a question. She is nobody's fool. She wittily prods the long-winded Polonius to stop being so wordy and get to the point: "More matter with less art." He says, but does not know as she does, that “brevity is the soul of wit”—that is, “wit” in its old sense of intelligence and discernment, not just cleverness.

Though she is sinfully married to her brother-in-law and has weaknesses both for sexual indulgence and drink, she carries herself with dignity and has insight into other people. Her sympathy for Ophelia, who she hoped would marry her son, is especially touching. She is also aware that Hamlet’s grief for his father’s death is excessive and spiritually unhealthy, even dangerous.

For most of the play, Hamlet wrongly believes that Gertrude helped Claudius kill his father, which is why he is tempted to kill her. This disastrous sin and crime is barely averted when Hamlet sees, at the moment of Polonius’s

Gertrude and her son, Hamlet, in the 1996 film adaptation

death, that she is astonished at his suspicion; she is not even aware that Claudius is guilty of murdering her first husband. Hamlet still heaps abuse on her, but now it is merely for marrying Claudius; he has to drop the charge of murder that had weighed so heavily on his mind.

Gertrude tries to be loyal to both her son and her husband. The situation is painful and extremely confusing for her. Hamlet appears to be insane, killing Polonius and talking to a ghost that is invisible to her, but she wants to protect him as best she can from Claudius's wrath after the "bloody deed." At any rate, we do her serious wrong to dismiss her as the "dull and shallow woman" so many critics have accused her of being. She mediates between the warring men in her life with great skill, and we have to try to imagine the tangled situation as it must appear to her. Naturally she would prefer to believe that Claudius played no role in her first husband's death and that he has no designs on her son's life, but when she realizes that she has drunk poisoned wine, the horrible truth instantly becomes clear to her, and her dying words try to warn Hamlet.

Horatio

Horatio is Hamlet's only close friend, his fellow student from Wittenberg, and Hamlet's model of self-possession and rational behavior. He is not "passion's slave"; his volatile friend envies and admires Horatio's perfect calm, which breaks briefly only when he realizes that Hamlet is about to die. But Hamlet dissuades Horatio from suicide by urging him to live and tell the world the full story, which only he will know.

Horatio is no yes-man or flatterer. He is quite ready to rebuke his royal friend when Hamlet is out of control. During

Hamlet and Horatio in the 2009 BBC production of the play

the graveyard fight with Laertes he says sharply, "Good my lord, be quiet!" On other occasions his quiet wisdom is felt even when he says little. He is notably restrained when Hamlet exults after the play has destroyed Claudius's composure. We sense that he knows Hamlet has botched an opportunity by letting his emotions get the better of him. When Hamlet muses on mortality in the graveyard, Horatio tells him he is dwelling "too curiously" on the morbid. He is also quietly shocked when Hamlet proudly relates how he arranged the deaths of Rosencrantz and Guildenstern.

Though Hamlet wants to believe the Ghost, Horatio is not so sure. He warns Hamlet about the danger of following it, and he proves to be right. He has no illusions about anyone. It is the cool Horatio, not the raging Ghost, whom Hamlet should have listened to.

Polonius

Polonius exemplifies the corruption of Claudius's court. He is an incurable snoop, cynical, and amoral. He even spies on his own children. His suspicious nature spoils the blossoming love of Hamlet and Ophelia, and he sends his servant Reynaldo to keep an eye on Laertes in Paris, blackening Laertes's character if necessary in order to elicit information.

Polonius's judgment is poor. He cannot give up the idea that Ophelia's rejection has driven Hamlet mad, though Claudius quickly sees that this is nonsense and that Hamlet is dangerous. The duel of wits between Claudius and Hamlet goes completely over the old man's head.

Polonius loves the sound of his own voice. Vainly garrulous, he tries to control every situation. Gertrude tries to make him get to the point ("More matter with less art," she orders him tartly), but she should have saved her breath; he will not be silenced.

He has no real interest in the theater; he despises the actors, despite Hamlet's warning that they may have the last word on men like him: "After your death you were better have a bad epitaph than their ill report while you live." Though Polonius sees that Hamlet is behaving outrageously during the play, he fails to grasp what is really going on; he still thinks Hamlet is preoccupied with Ophelia.

Why does Hamlet seem to hate the relatively harmless old Polonius more than the man who has murdered his father and debauched his mother? We are left to wonder, though Polonius is certainly a vexing figure.

When he insists on eavesdropping on Gertrude and her son, urging her to be severe, he is, as usual, out of his depth, and the result is his death. Until he kills Polonius, Hamlet is gaining the upper hand over his real enemy, Claudius; but then the balance of power shifts against him. He treats the corpse with complete contempt. "I'll lug the guts into the neighbor room," he tells Gertrude, and when Rosencrantz and Guildenstern demand to know where Hamlet has hidden the body, he says sarcastically that its odor will eventually guide them.

Laertes

His father's son, Laertes is a shallow playboy who has obviously not gone to Paris to study the questions that have drawn Hamlet and Horatio to Wittenberg. Polonius is proud of the boy, whatever his vices; Ophelia, though innocent and pious herself, is wise to him.

When he learns of his father's death, Laertes reacts in a flash, without anguished soliloquies. He wants revenge—at once. The contrast between him and Hamlet could hardly be more stark:

> ***To hell, allegiance! Vows to the blackest devil!***
> ***Conscience and grace to the profoundest pit!***
> ***I dare damnation.***

Laertes has no illusions about the diabolical nature of revenge, but he could not care less. He is not the man to admire a calm Horatio. He defies Gertrude's plea for him to be calm: "That drop of blood that's calm proclaims me bastard!" He is indeed "passion's slave," and he is proud of it.

Laertes and Hamlet duel in the 1996 film production of the play.

And yet, at bottom, his fury is merely a distilled version of Hamlet's first response to the Ghost, when the prince vowed that the Ghost's command would live "all alone" in his mind, "unmixed with baser matter." But whereas Hamlet found himself unable to sustain an obsession with revenge, Laertes finds it natural. He would be willing "to cut [Hamlet's] throat i'th' church." And he is ready to stoop to treachery in order to get even. He is even more enraged when he sees Ophelia insane and then learns that she has drowned.

Even Laertes has his limits, though. When the plot to kill Hamlet with the poisoned foil is on the verge of being executed, he admits to himself, "And yet it is almost against my conscience."

Almost. Then, suddenly, everything goes wrong. The foils are exchanged, Laertes is fatally wounded, and the queen drinks the poisoned wine that was meant for Hamlet. In the ensuing uproar Laertes confesses everything, blames the king, and begs Hamlet for forgiveness, which is readily given.

"Sweets to the sweet: farewell!"

In the end we, too, absolve and forgive Laertes. He has been cruelly wronged, tenderly cares for his poor sister, and, though used cynically by Claudius, has turned out to be a far better man than his father.

Ophelia

Due to the purity and innocence that the corrupt court loves her for, Ophelia is repeatedly used and controlled by men: her father orders her to cease all contact with Hamlet and makes her his spy. She is condemned for being "weak" even as she is praised for her good and gentle nature.

Ophelia always means well. There is not a speck of malice or cunning in her. Everyone in the corrupt court loves her for her purity and innocence. Gertrude hoped she would marry Hamlet, and even Claudius is touched by her madness and death—despite her apparent suicide, he orders the church to give her a normal funeral.

When Hamlet insults her, she really thinks he has gone mad. She remembers him as a model gentleman, courtier, scholar, and soldier, and cannot explain his violent change to her except as a baffling explosion of insanity.

Mignon Nevada as Ophelia in the 1910 Hamlet opera

When, at the play, his taunts become downright obscene, she scolds him mildly, trying to insist on a little decency, but he ignores her objections. He is too angry to consider what she deserves.

The next time we see her, her mind has snapped. Her father has been slain, her brother is gone, and Hamlet has turned against her, She is alone and friendless. The furies of the men around her have destroyed her; she knows nothing of the Ghost and the murder, of course. No wonder she drowns herself.

Sent to England, Hamlet escapes and returns to Denmark just in time to see Ophelia's funeral procession. This is his first notice of her death; he is shocked. His love for her comes flooding back. He vies with Laertes in extravagant professions of love for her, but he still fails to see his own role in her destruction. Though she is the most innocent victim of his tragic quest for revenge, he never reflects on what it has done to them both. Like Laertes, he is willing to see the innocent destroyed along with the guilty. Masculine hatred consumes feminine love.

Although Ophelia is the most innocent victim in Hamlet's tragic quest for revenge, he never reflects on what it has done to her. He only sees Ophelia in terms of what she represents to him: first a love interest, and then a traitor, and then a symbol of his own passion.

Chapter Three

A Closer Look

Themes

The Consequences of Revenge

Revenge is the chief theme of *Hamlet*. The play explores the elusive difference between punishment and getting even. Hamlet hates his uncle even before learning that Claudius has murdered his father, an apparently simple fact that Hamlet feels he must prove before he proceeds to avenge it.

Hamlet's emotions are as complicated as they are powerful, and he has our full sympathy as he tries to consider every angle of this baffling task, which tests his immense intelligence. His own life may be at stake, and so is his immortal soul. The wrong answer may bring about his eternal damnation.

The 1996 Kenneth Branagh film adaptation of Hamlet

The Inevitability of Death

From the Ghost's first appearance to the final scene, with such seemingly digressive episodes as the exhuming of Yorick's skull before Ophelia's burial, we are seldom allowed to forget about death. Mortality pervades this play like no other. As Gertrude puts it, "All that lives must die/Passing through nature to eternity."

Mortality receives many elaborations, such as Hamlet's morbid joke to Claudius that "a man may fish with the worm that hath eat of a king, and eat of the fish that hath fed of that worm," so that "a king may go a progress through the guts of a beggar." Similarly, he broods caustically on "the noble dust of Alexander" (the Great), and likewise on "Imperious Caesar, dead and turned to clay."

The Ambiguity of Religious Doctrine

Death, the final divorce of body and soul, brings us to the theme of religion. Four quick mentions of the university at Wittenberg, where Hamlet and Horatio have studied together, alert us that both young men must be well aware of the new doctrines of Protestantism that were born there. The disputes between Catholics and Protestants were an extremely sensitive subject in Elizabethan England, whose official church stood somewhere between the Pope and the Puritans, banning any explicit affirmation of purgatory.

Shakespeare evades this problem by counting on his audience to pick up his allusions. When the ambiguous Ghost says that its sins are being "purged" in fire, the Bard leaves the inference up to viewers and readers. And when the Ghost complains that it has died without the sacraments, we again have to draw our own conclusions.

Hamlet comes upon Claudius praying.

Shakespeare plays on religious uncertainties, tantalizing us with "Thoughts beyond the reaches of our souls." After the play scene, Hamlet finds his uncle on his knees, seemingly praying. Is this an apt moment to take his revenge? Full revenge would require killing him during the commission of his sins, thus sending him straight to hell. So Hamlet delays once more.

Later, Hamlet sends Rosencrantz and Guildenstern to die like his father, without the final sacraments, and when Laertes curses him in the graveyard—"The devil take thy soul!"—he instantly retorts, "Thou prayest not well." True enough, but it amounts to the same prayer Hamlet has been saying as he seeks to damn his enemies.

Hamlet is steeped in Christian language, concepts, and symbols. It mentions or alludes to God, Jesus, Adam, Cain, Jeptha, King Herod, Saint Patrick, Saint Valentine, original sin, angels, devils, Doomsday, the Last Trumpet, salvation, damnation, heaven, hell, purgatory, prayers, and more. Ophelia, always pious, becomes even more religious in her madness.

At once deeply Christian and just as deeply baffling, the play never fully commits itself to either a Catholic or a Protestant position, leaving us to wonder where the ultimate truth lies.

Motifs

In his first soliloquy, Hamlet reveals that he is revolted and disgusted by "all the uses of this world." The play keeps echoing his dark estimate of what he finally, on the verge of his own death, calls "this harsh world."

As he tells Polonius, in a more bantering vein, "To be honest, as this world goes, is to be one man picked out of ten thousand." Yet he sincerely means what he says. Claudius, trying to repent for his own terrible sins, contrasts this world with the next one:

In the corrupted currents of this world,
Offense's gilded hand may shove by justice,
And oft 'tis seen the wicked prize itself
Buys out the law. But 'tis not so above …

He is thinking specifically of himself. In this corrupt world, he is saying, the guilty rich man may bribe his way to power and success, just as he has done, even using the very crown he has stolen to buy off others, but it is otherwise in heaven, where hypocrisy is impossible and God sees the moral quality of our actions without their earthly disguises.

Others are also well aware of the double standards that prevail in this sinful world. The two gravediggers agree that Ophelia, who committed suicide, is being allowed a proper Christian funeral only because of her high social rank. Otherwise, one of these poor men remarks, she would have been buried in disgrace at the crossroads, like other suicides. The other concurs: "And the more pity that great folk should have countenance in this world to drown or hang themselves more than their even-Christen" (i.e., their fellow Christians). His protest may sound a little absurd put this way, but he has a point.

The pitiless priest who conducts the funeral echoes that point: the way Ophelia died was "doubtful," he says, and only the king's decree has overruled normal church procedure for suicides ("great command o'ersways the order," as he says).

Related to this is the motif of hypocrisy, which is signaled in various ways. Hamlet (quite unfairly) blames Ophelia for all the false pretenses of her gender: "I have heard of your paintings too, well enough: God hath given you one face, and you make yourselves another." His final comment on this subject is his mock order to Yorick's skull: "Now get you to my lady's chamber, and tell her, let her paint an inch thick, to this favor she must come." That is, no matter how much makeup she applies, she will end up with a face like Yorick's. (He says this before he knows that Ophelia is already dead.)

Against, or supplementing, the play's religious themes is its motif of classical learning from pagan antiquity. There are collections of both its historical and its mythological figures. The historical include Caesar and Alexander, of course, as well as Brutus, Nero, and sites such as the Roman Capitol, Mount Olympus, Pelion, and Ossa. The names Claudius and Horatio are Roman, too; Horatio, trying to kill himself, actually says he is "more an antique Roman than a Dane."

We also hear of many pagan gods: Jove (king of the gods); Hyperion, also called Phoebus (the sun god); Mars (god of war); Hymen (god of marriage); Neptune (the sea god); Hecate (goddess of witchcraft); Tellus (Earth's goddess); Vulcan (the gods' blacksmith); and the mighty Hercules, the horrid Cyclops, the grieving Niobe, and fearsome beasts such as the Nemean lion and the Hyrcanian tiger. The destruction of Troy, or Ilium, is recounted, too, as narrated by Virgil's Aeneas to Queen Dido, with recollections of the slaughter of King Priam by "the rugged Pyrrhus," son of Achilles, and the uncontrollable grief of Priam's piteous queen, Hecuba. The Trojan Horse merits a brief allusion. The Ghost also speaks of Lethe, the river of forgetfulness in Hades.

All this classical lore adds further volume and resonance to the play's rich language. It also distracts us from the Christian setting of Denmark, and it enables Hamlet to exalt his father in heroic terms, avoiding the fatal subject of the "foul crimes" for which the Ghost is being punished.

Another important motif in Hamlet is the relation between memory and purpose. The Ghost commands Hamlet, "Remember me," and Hamlet swears he will do so, erasing everything else from "the book and volume of my brain." During his verbal assault on Gertrude, the Ghost has to return to remind him, "Do not forget," chiding him for "thy almost blunted purpose." In the play scene, the Player King (whose speeches make shrewd comments on the "real" action of the play), observes:

> ***Purpose is but the***
> ***slave to memory,***
> ***Of violent birth, but***
> ***poor validity.***

His thought is echoed when Claudius says to Laertes that "love is begun by time," and that "time qualifies the spark and fire of it." If we fail to act quickly on our love, time may dissipate our will to do so.

Symbols

Denmark's evil is symbolized by the poison Claudius chooses for his murders, which turns out to be an evil he is unable to control. He finally manages to arrange Hamlet's death, but he himself dies of poisoning, too, along with Gertrude and Laertes. Again and again, the play shows men unable to control their passions and the natural consequences of their actions.

There are several references to poison and venom. Slander and calumny (hurtful misrepresentations) are said to be poisonous in their effects. Hamlet is said to be "envenomed" with envy of Laertes; he assures the king that the actors merely "poison in jest."

Another figurative form of poison is drunkenness. In the first scene in which he appears, Claudius drinks, as he loves to do, to the sound of cannons roaring. Hamlet finds this disgusting. He welcomes Horatio to Elsinore with the wry promise, "We'll teach you to drink deep ere you depart." That night, as they await the Ghost, they hear the cannons roar again. Hamlet explains that this is a Danish custom, albeit one he considers "more honored in the breach than the observance." This "heavy-headed revel," he says, has earned the Danes a "swinish" international reputation as a country of drunkards. There is further evidence of Claudius's addiction to drink later in the play, but the baneful tradition clearly did not begin with him; presumably Hamlet's father had his share in it, too.

Denmark's sins are further conveyed to us by Shakespeare's rich imagery of disease and malady. Terms such as sick, disease, infection, ulcer (or imposthume), pleurisy, apoplexed, leprous, corruption, cicatrice (scar), and hectic (fever) recur time and again. The aging king of Norway, uncle of Fortinbras, is "bedrid"; corpses are "rotten," "pocky" (syphilitic), and foul-smelling. "How long will a man lie in the earth ere he rot?" Hamlet asks the gravedigger. Joking about his pretended madness, he says, "My wit's diseased." The language of pathology and medicine is offset by the occasional use of such terms as health and wholesome, but our chief and most powerful impression is of a deeply diseased world typified by Denmark, where "something is rotten."

There are more things in
heaven and earth, Horatio,
Than are dreamt of in your philosophy.

Dreams themselves are part of this reality. Hamlet says, "O God, I could be bounded in a nutshell and count myself a king of infinite space, were it not that I have bad dreams" and "To sleep, perchance to dream."

Language

Dozens of *Hamlet*'s lines and phrases are familiar to readers. Here is a sampling:

"A little more than kin, and less than kind." "To thine own self be true." "Murder most foul." "The time is out of joint." "Brevity is the soul of wit." "Though this be madness, yet there is method in it." "The play's the thing." "To be or not to be: that is the question." "The slings and arrows of outrageous fortune." "To sleep, perchance to dream; ay, there's the rub." "The undiscovered country from whose bourn no traveler returns "Alas, poor Yorick!" "Sweets to the sweet!"

Today the term "rhetoric" suggests empty, inflated, speech. In Shakespeare's day, the art of persuasion was a respectable field of study. Shakespeare understood that the kind of plain language we prize today is itself only one form of rhetoric.

Shakespeare on Facebook?

SHAKESPEARE'S PLAYS HAVE been shared through almost every medium imaginable, including social media.

In 2013, Isinglass, a Chicago-based theater company "staged" *Much Ado About Nothing* entirely on Facebook. The comedy was particularly fitting for the social media platform because it has to do with characters distributing information—or, for the most part, misinformation. The director, John Zajac, said he started the project because he wanted to explore how people use social media platforms like Facebook to create and share their own stories with the world.

"Actors" used their personal social media accounts to impersonate Beatrice, Benedick, and the others, updating their statuses in real time to reflect the events of the play. They wrote the posts in modern English to make them as accessible as could be, and encouraged their friends to comment freely and share, involving as many people as possible.

Isinglass plans to follow up its production of *Much Ado* with *The Tempest*. Rather than using Facebook, the theater company is creating a virtual world where online audiences can take on the roles of characters in *The Tempest* and inhabit Prospero's island. The project is intended to explore the blurring of the lines between fantasy and reality, a question the characters in *The Tempest* are forced to confront themselves. It also draws parallels to online games, where players feel empowered to be anything they want.

Shakespeare never could have foreseen the creation of the Internet or realized that in the twenty-first century his words would be distributed more easily than ever before. As his verses reveal a concern with the plight of the common person, it is more than plausible that he would be pleased to know that more people than ever are enjoying his work in new ways.

The Isinglass theater's "Social Shakespeare" productions merge the Bard's words with social media.

Interpreting the Play

Hamlet and the Critics

Serious criticism and scholarship of the play began in the middle of the eighteenth century. The versatile English writer Samuel Johnson singled out Hamlet as the greatest of Shakespeare's plays for its sheer "variety" and abundance of character and incident.

In the twentieth century, Andrew Cecil Bradley, the most influential of all Shakespeare critics, wrote that Hamlet is a man quite capable of action, but his will is paralyzed by "melancholy," or emotional depression, brought on by the shock of his father's death and his mother's remarriage.

John Dover Wilson's 1935 book *What Happens in Hamlet*, offered a close scene-by-scene analysis of the play and had much effect on how it was staged and acted for some years. Sigmund Freud argued that the prince is the victim of an Oedipus complex that gives him a guilty sympathy with Claudius and inhibits him from taking revenge. As Freud saw it, Hamlet had a secret wish to kill his father and sleep with his mother, so he could not bring himself to kill the man who had only done what he wished to do. Laurence Olivier adopted the psychoanalytic view (as well as some of Dover Wilson's ideas) in his 1948 film of the play.

In his posthumous 1951 book *The Meaning of Shakespeare*, Harold Clarke Goddard rejected the whole premise of nearly all previous Hamlet criticism. Goddard argued that Hamlet's delay is due to his conscience: he knows that the Ghost's demand for revenge is evil.

Later studies, such as those of Northrop Frye and Stephen Booth, have inclined back toward the older view that revenge is Hamlet's moral duty. Maynard Mack, in his highly regarded essay "The World of *Hamlet*," sees the play as taking place in a realm of ultimate and irresolvable mystery, where the great questions the prince faces defy final answers.

CHRONOLOGY

1564 William Shakespeare is born, presumably, on April 23 in Stratford-upon-Avon, England

1578–1582 Span of Shakespeare's "Lost Years," covering the time between leaving school and marrying Anne Hathaway of Stratford

1582 At age eighteen, Shakespeare marries Anne Hathaway, age twenty-six, on November 28

1583 Susanna Shakespeare, William and Anne's first child, is born in May, six months after the wedding

1584 Birth of twins Hamnet and Judith Shakespeare

1585–1592 Shakespeare leaves his family in Stratford to become an actor and playwright in a London theater company

1587 Public beheading of Mary Queen of Scots

1593–1594 The Bubonic (Black) Plague closes theaters in London

1594–1596 As a leading playwright, Shakespeare creates some of his most popular works, including *A Midsummer Night's Dream* and *Romeo and Juliet*

1596 Hamnet Shakespeare dies in August at age eleven, possibly of plague

1596–1597 *The Merchant of Venice* and *Henry IV, Part One* are most likely written

1599 The Globe Theatre opens

1600 *Julius Caesar* is first performed at the Globe

1600–1601 *Hamlet* is believed to have been written

1601–1602 *Twelfth Night* is probably composed

1603 Queen Elizabeth I dies; Scottish king James VI succeeds her and becomes England's James I

1604 Shakespeare pens *Othello*

1605 *Macbeth* is composed

1608–1610 London's theaters are forced to close when the plague returns and kills an estimated thirty-three thousand people

1611 *The Tempest* is written

1613 The Globe Theatre is destroyed by fire

1614 The reopening of the Globe

1616 Shakespeare dies on April 23

1623 Anne Hathaway, Shakespeare's widow, dies; a collection of Shakespeare's plays, known as the First Folio, is published

A SHAKESPEARE GLOSSARY

addition A name or title, such as knight, duke, duchess, king, etc.

affect To like or love; to be attracted to.

approve To prove or confirm.

attend To pay attention.

belike Probably.

beseech To beg or request.

bondman A slave.

bootless Futile; useless; in vain.

broil A battle.

charge Expense, responsibility; to command or accuse.

common A term describing the common people, below nobility.

condition Social rank; quality.

countenance Face; appearance; favor.

cousin A relative.

curious Careful; attentive to detail.

discourse To converse; conversation.

discover To reveal or uncover.

dispatch To speed or hurry; to send; to kill.

doubt To suspect.

entreat To beg or appeal.

envy To hate or resent; hatred; resentment.

ere Before.

eyne Eyes.

fain Gladly.

fare To eat; to prosper.

favor Face, privilege.

fellow A peer or equal.

filial Of a child toward its parent.

fine An end; "in fine" means in sum.

folio A book made up of individually printed sheets, each folded in half to make four pages. Shakespeare's folios contain all of his known plays in addition to other works.

fond Foolish.

fool A darling.

genius A good or evil spirit.

gentle Well-bred; not common.

gentleman One whose labor was done by servants. (Note: to call someone a *gentleman* was not a mere compliment on his manners; it meant that he was above the common people.)

gentles People of quality.

get To beget (a child).

go to "Go on"; "come off it."

go we Let us go.

haply Perhaps.

happily By chance; fortunately.

hard by Nearby.

heavy Sad or serious.

husbandry Thrift; economy.

instant Immediate.

kind One's nature; species.

knave A villain; a poor man.

lady A woman of high social rank. (Note: *lady* was not a synonym for *woman* or *polite woman*; it was not a compliment but simply a word referring to one's actual legal status in society, like *gentleman*.)

leave Permission; "take my leave" means depart (with permission).

lief, lieve "I had as lief" means I would just as soon; I would rather.

like To please; "it likes me not" means it is disagreeable to me.

livery The uniform of a nobleman's servants; emblem.

Lord Chamberlain's Men The company of players Shakespeare joined in London; under James I they became the King's Men.

mark Notice; pay attention.

morrow Morning.

needs Necessarily.

nice Too fussy or fastidious.

owe To own.

passing Very.

peculiar Individual; exclusive.

privy Private; secret.

proper Handsome; one's very own ("his proper son").

protest To insist or declare.

quite Completely.

require Request.

several Different, various.

severally Separately.

sirrah A term used to address social inferiors.

sooth Truth.

state Condition; social rank.

still Always; persistently.

success Result(s).

surfeit Fullness.

touching Concerning; about; as for.

translate To transform.

unfold To disclose.

verse Writing that uses a regular metrical rhythm and is divided from other lines by a space.

villain A low or evil person; originally, a peasant.

voice A vote; consent; approval.

vouchsafe To confide or grant.

vulgar Common.

want To lack.

weeds Clothing.

what ho "Hello, there!"

wherefore Why.

wit Intelligence; sanity.

withal Moreover; nevertheless.

without Outside.

would Wish.

SUGGESTED ESSAY TOPICS

1. Describe Hamlet's inner conflicts about religion and revenge, and how these conflicts make *Hamlet* a true drama. Support your answer using specific examples from the text.

2. Did Hamlet truly love Ophelia? How do you know? Support your answer using specific examples from the text.

3. Gertrude, Hamlet's mother, has traditionally been seen as an oblivious, passive, sensual woman. How is this judgment problematic? What alternative lenses can we use to interpret her character? Support your answer using specific examples from the text.

4. Compare and contrast Horatio and Hamlet. How does Hamlet's character highlight Horatio's, and vice versa? Support your answer using specific examples from the text.

TEST YOUR MEMORY

1. What country is threatening to invade Denmark?
   a) England; b) Norway; c) Poland; d) Germany

2. Where have Hamlet and Horatio gone to school?
   a) Paris; b) Wittenberg; c) Oxford; d) Cambridge

3. Why does Polonius send Reynaldo to Paris?
   a) To attend the university; b) To borrow money; c) To follow Hamlet; d) To spy on Laertes

4. What vice are the Danes notorious for?
   a) drunkenness; b) quarreling; c) gambling; d) smoking

5. How does the Ghost say he was murdered?
   a) poison; b) stabbing c) strangling d) hired assassination

6. Whom do the king and queen ask to get to the bottom of Hamlet's strange behavior?
   a) Ophelia; b) Horatio; c) Laertes; d) Rosencrantz and Guildenstern

7. During Hamlet's play, what fictional woman does the First Player weep for?
   a) Helen of Troy; b) Andromache; c) Hecuba; d) Penelope

8. What is the "undiscovered country" to which Hamlet refers?
a) love; b) death; c) purgatory; d) ignorance

9. How do Claudius and Gertrude react to the news that Hamlet wants them to attend a play?
a) They welcome it as evidence that he is normal again;
b) They are dismayed; c) Gertrude is glad, but Claudius is suspicious; d) They want to know more about the play

10. Where does Hamlet tell Ophelia to go?
a) home; b) to hell; c) to a nunnery; d) to Paris

11. How does Ophelia take Hamlet's harsh language to her?
a) It makes her furious; b) She is mystified; c) It convinces her that he is really insane; d) She prays for him

12. What is the purpose of acting, according to Hamlet?
a) To imitate nature; b) To win awards; c) To earn a profit;
d) To inspire social reform

13. What quality does Hamlet most admire in Horatio?
a) His intelligence; b) His scholarship; c) His courage;
d) His patience

14. What is the actual title of the play Hamlet calls *The Mousetrap*?
a) *The Revenger's Tragedy*; b) *The Murder of Gonzago*;
c) *Oedipus Rex*; d) *The Fall of Troy*

15. When Hamlet finds Claudius on his knees, what reason does he give for sparing his life?
a) He is afraid of sending him to heaven; b) There has been too much bloodshed already; c) He wants to give him another chance; d) He hopes Laertes will kill him

16. Why is Hamlet reluctant to see his mother alone?
a) He fears a scolding; b) He is tempted to kill her; c) She knows about the murder of his father; d) He will have to tell her the full truth about Claudius

17. Where is Hamlet going when the pirates capture him?
a) He is fleeing Claudius; b) He is being sent to England; c) He is returning to Wittenberg; d) He is on his way to meet Fortinbras.

18. What was the name of the court jester Hamlet knew as a child?
a) Yorick; b) Osric; c) Benedick; d) Dogberry.

19. Why would Ophelia be denied a normal funeral?
a) Because of the king's command; b) Because of her family's influence; c) Because her death may have been a suicide; d) Because of her association with Hamlet.

20. Who ultimately becomes king of Denmark?
a) Horatio; b) Laertes; c) Fortinbras; d) Donalbain.

Answer Key

1. b; 2. b; 3. d; 4. a; 5. a; 6. d; 7. c; 8. b; 9. a; 10. c; 11. c; 12. a; 13. d; 14. b; 15. a; 16. b; 17. b; 18. a; 19. c; 20. c.

FURTHER INFORMATION

Books

Ackroyd, Peter. *Shakespeare: The Biography*. New York: Nan A. Talese, 2005.

Dunton-Downer, Leslie, and Alan Riding. *The Essential Shakespeare Handbook*. New York: Dorling Kindersley, 2004.

Folger Shakespeare Library. *Hamlet*. New York: Washington Square Press, 2004.

Manga Shakespeare series. *Hamlet*. New York: Harry N. Abrams/ Amulet, 2007.

Websites

Absolute Shakespeare

www.absoluteshakespeare.com

Absolute Shakespeare is a resource for the Bard's plays, sonnets, and poems, and includes summaries, quotes, films, trivia, and more.

Play Shakespeare

www.playshakespeare.com

The Ultimate Free Shakespeare Resource features all the play texts with an online glossary, reviews, a discussion forum, and links to festivals worldwide.

Films

Hamlet, BBC production; starring Derek Jacobi as Hamlet and Patrick Stewart as Claudius, 1980.

Hamlet, Broadway production; starring Richard Burton, videotaped in 1964 and transferred to DVD.

Hamlet, directed by Franco Zeffirelli; starring Mel Gibson as Hamlet and Helena Bonham Carter as Ophelia, 1990.

Hamlet, directed by Laurence Olivier; starring Olivier as Hamlet, 1948.

Hamlet, directed by Michael Almereyda; starring Ethan Hawke as Hamlet, Julia Stiles as Ophelia, and Bill Murray as Polonius, 2000.

William Shakespeare's Hamlet, directed by Kenneth Branagh; starring Branagh as Hamlet, Derek Jacobi as Claudius, and Kate Winslet as Ophelia, 1996.

BIBLIOGRAPHY

"Bard's 'Cursed' Tomb is Revamped." BBC News, May 28, 2008. Accessed May 5, 2015. http://news.bbc.co.uk/2/hi/uk_news/england/coventry_warwickshire/7422986.stm.

Bate, Jonathan, and Eric Rasmussen, eds. *William Shakespeare Complete Works* (Modern Library). New York: Random House, 2007.

Bloom, Harold. Shakespeare: *The Invention of the Human*. New York: Riverhead Books, 1998.

Burgess, Anthony. *Shakespeare*. New York: Alfred A. Knopf, 1970.

Chute, Marchette. *Shakespeare of London*. New York: Dutton, 1949.

Dobson, Michael, and Stanley Wells, eds. *The Oxford Companion to Shakespeare*. New York: Oxford University Press, 2008.

Garber, Marjorie. *Shakespeare After All*. New York: Pantheon, 2004.

Goddard, Harold C. *The Meaning of Shakespeare*. Chicago: University of Chicago Press, 1951.

Greenblatt, Stephen. *Will in the World: How Shakespeare Became Shakespeare*. New York: W. W. Norton & Company, 2004.

Griggs, Brandon, and Lucy Pawle. "Research Suggests Shakespeare Wrote 'Lost' Play." CNN, April 10, 2015. Accessed May 7, 2015. http://www.cnn.com/2015/04/10/entertainment/shakespeare-playdouble-falsehood-feat.

Honan, Park. Shakespeare: A Life. New York: Oxford University Press, 1998.

Levitt, Aimee. "Social Media Shakespeare: An Idea Whose Time Has Finally Come." The Chicago Reader, May 2, 2013.Accessed May 8, 2015. http://www.chicagoreader.com/Bleader/archives/2013/05/02/social-media-shakespearean-idea-whose-time-has-finally-come.

Schoenbaum, Samuel. William *Shakespeare: A Documentary Life*. New York: Oxford University Press, 1975.

———. *William Shakespeare: Records and Images*. New York: Oxford University Press, 1981.

Traversi, D. L. *An Approach to Shakespeare*. Palo Alto, CA: Stanford University Press, 1957.

Van Doren, Mark. *Shakespeare*. Garden City, NY: Doubleday, 1939.

INDEX

Page numbers in **boldface** are illustrations.

ABOUT THE AUTHOR

Caitlyn Christensen is a writer and editor located in Pittsburgh, Pennsylvania. More of her work is available at www.caitlynlucechristensen.com.